MANIPULATION AND DARK PSYCHOLOGY

Improve the Quality of Your Life. The New Guide to Learn the Effects of Mental Manipulation and Dark Psychology, Speed Read People and Defend Yourself Psychologically

JACK BROWN

© Copyright 2020 - All rights reserved.

Table of Contents

Introduction

To recognize how manipulation works, it is important to understand the mechanisms of the human mind. The unconscious mind makes up almost all of the brain's functions. It controls your breathing, digestion, heart rate, etc. It is home to your creativity and imagination and memories. It is also used to build your automatic response to feeling threatened. Your emotions are also present in the unconscious mind.

The psychology behind manipulation focuses on the idea that instead of making someone do what you want them to do, it is the key to make another person want to do what you want them to do. How a manipulator can make this happen is through understanding the person they are trying to manipulate. The genuine wants and desires of the person being manipulated must be learned so that the manipulator can modify said wants and desires to match their own goals. The most important thing a manipulator should keep in mind is that the closer they are to the person being manipulated, the easier it will be to manipulate them.

One of the most common forms of manipulation comes in the form of emotional and psychological manipulation. Psychological manipulation focuses on the unevenness of power between people. The individual with the power preys on the weaknesses of the other person. The cycle of this form of manipulation is that the manipulator finds an individual's weaknesses. The manipulator takes advantage of said weaknesses, and then the process continues to repeat. Once a manipulator successfully manipulates a person, they are not likely to stop manipulating until being forced to stop.

While it can be difficult to notice when one is being manipulated and stop someone from manipulating, there are ways to protect one's mind from manipulation. One tool that can be helpful is meditation. When a person can silence their mind and become more grounded, it can be noticeably easier to deal with emotional and psychological manipulation. Even when other people are hostile and controlling, an individual with inner peace can remain calm but aware of the manipulator's intentions. Avoiding an emotional attachment to manipulative people is also crucial. This approach can be challenging, especially if the manipulator shows false signs of kindness to gain a person's trust. The best way to weed out the manipulators is to pay attention to any beginning signs that someone is overpowering someone emotionally. Once there is any warning of emotional manipulation, it is time to slowly back out of the relationship before attachment forms.

A manipulative person strives for power over another person. And so, by not allowing the manipulator into one's head, the manipulator loses its power. An individual can prevent a manipulator from getting into their heads by laughing at their insults or statements and going along with what they say without agreeing with what is said. It is also extremely important to focus on one's idea of self rather than how others see them. When a person has a solid sense of self-worth, it becomes nearly impossible for others to weaken that self-assurance. One finally, a tool that can be used to stop manipulation is escaping from harmful relationships. People cannot be forced to change; it is best to save oneself from toxic relationships before the physical and emotional threat becomes too dangerous. Every person deserves to be in relationships where they are valued rather than break a person down.

To prevent manipulation, one must first become aware of the signs of manipulation. One of the most common red flags that manipulation is taking place is if an individual is feeling guilty. Manipulators thrive on making the people around them feel bad about themselves. Since manipulators cannot own up to their faults, they tend to blame other people, which creates guilt for the person being manipulated. This is commonly known in abusive relationships when the abuser says that the victim made them act aggressively. A manipulator's victim will truly believe that it is their fault and stay in the toxic relationship. A manipulator will also use the controlled person's words to gain power and enforce the guilt approach.

Once all of the signs of manipulative behavior have been comprehended, it becomes important to understand the power of emotion in connection to manipulation. An individual's emotions play a vital role in one's ability to manipulate and to be manipulated. Emotion is one of the main tools used in manipulation. Manipulators will use an emotional connection to get as much information from another person as possible. This is also the main outlet of learning the weaknesses of the individual being manipulated. Additionally, manipulators will fake emotion to strategically undermine a person's decisions and create a level of self-consciousness. If a person's sudden onset of emotion does not appear genuine, call them out or get out of the relationship.

Sometimes it may take time for an individual to pick up on the warning signs of manipulation. However, one can train the brain to notice seemly innocent words and actions that can lead to manipulation. It may seem flattering if a partner wants to know what the other person is up to. However, when a boyfriend or girlfriend is constantly asking what the other person is doing and becomes angry when they do not receive an answer, this should send off a warning sign in the head. This can indicate that the partner monitors their significant other and can even go as far as to turn into stalking.

A question that is often wondered by people who hear of someone having been in an abusive relationship is how could they have stayed with the person? An abuser manipulates their partner into staying by providing moments of love. The abuser attempts to reel their partner in again after moments of violence by providing compliments or gifts. The brain needs to recognize that this does not mean the abuse will stop; it is only a ploy to make the person stay. Get out of the relationship as quickly as possible.

Abusers are also aware that many people draw the line at physical abuse. It can be more difficult to detect psychological abuse. However, there are still ways to train the mind to pick up on psychological trauma. Conversations surrounding jealousy can be a great indicator. If a partner is constantly jealous of their significant other spending time with other people, they are most likely trying to isolate their victim from everyone else. The manipulator is attempting to create a false notion that the partner can only rely on the manipulator.

Once an individual can train the mind to pick up on manipulative tendencies and phrases, it is time to get out of a manipulative situation altogether. The way an individual responds to manipulation depends on the type of manipulation that is taking place. If a person finds themselves in a situation where the manipulator is aggressive, for example, an abusive relationship, it is wise to speak with a professional about the best way to exit. Speaking to a therapist or a hotline specializing in domestic violence are two great tools to find the safest course of action.

If an individual is being manipulated but does not feel a sense of danger, either physically or emotionally, it becomes important not to allow the manipulator's words to sink in, let it go in one ear and out of the other. It is also strategic to create boundaries. Manipulators tend to create boundaries that are far too strict or too involved. It is helpful if the manipulated person responds by following their boundaries and disregarding the manipulators. One last response to manipulation is not to make any rash decisions.

Another approach to preventing or stopping oneself from being manipulated is to rewire the brain to be socially dominant. Studies have shown that social dominance is not improved by heightening the level of aggression or physical strength a person exerts. Instead, when an individual becomes more resilient, dominance can be achieved. When a person can find success in one area of their life, they can translate that mindset into other life instances. Additionally, attempting to transform oneself into an extrovert can be useful. Extroverts tend to exhibit high levels of social dominance. To become an extrovert, an individual must be open-minded. Some of the traits of an extrovert are perceived as negative, but focusing on the positive attributes can help a person develop some of the desirable character traits of an extrovert. Another way to look at extroverts positively is to think of influential people who are considered extroverts.

The next step is to practice the behaviors of an extrovert until they become natural. Specifically, look at opportunities to call attention to oneself is a beneficial way to learn to interact with all types of people. However, if an individual truly cannot be an extrovert, it is still possible to act the part. Plenty of famous actors pretend to be an extrovert on screen but are introverts behind the scenes. One example is Johnny Depp. The Hollywood star has played the roles of extroverts such as Willy Wonka and Captain Jack Sparrow. Still, in real life, Depp chooses to stay away from social situations.

Learning from others is another possible way to become an extrovert. There tends to be more than one personality type in a given group of people, including extroverts. Watch how the extroverts in the group act compared to themselves and replicate their behavior. One final option is to have a complete understanding of oneself. Once individuals know who they are, they can begin to look at how the people around them perceive them. This leads to a person's ability to see what attributes they have that other people respond to positively and which characters can still be improved. The extrovert is not as easily manipulated, which promotes the act of transforming, even if it's only on the surface, into an extrovert.

CHAPTER 1:

What is Manipulation?

Brainwashing and hypnosis are the two forms of mind control that easily come to mind. While these two are important to understanding mind control's functioning and how it all works, they are not the only available options. Others can be used and are often more effective in the short term than either brainwashing or hypnosis. These particular tactics can be used in everyday situations, for example, in normal conversations; a person may have with others.

The main thing to remember about the next three forms of mind control is that they are more likely to occur in a person's daily life with the people they know and trust. A person will not put their subject into isolation or force them into an altered state of mind as with brainwashing. Instead, they will employ different techniques to change the way their subject thinks. The three types of mind control that fit into this category include manipulation, persuasion, and deception. This chapter will discuss manipulation and how it can work to change the way "the subject" thinks. While manipulation may not put the person who is employing the tactic in harms' way or cause any immediate danger, it is set up to work in a deceptive and underhanded way to change the behavior, viewpoint, and perception that the intended subject has in regards to a particular topic or situation.

What Is Manipulation?

This book will deliberate and discuss manipulation in terms of psychological manipulation, defined as a social influence working to alter individuals' behaviors or perception, or the subject, through deceptive, abusive, or underhanded methods. The manipulator works to advance his interests, usually to the detriment of another. Hence, most of their techniques are considered deceptive, abusive, exploitative, and devious. Whereas social influence is not completely negative, when a group or an individual is being manipulated, there is the likelihood of causing them harm. Social influence, such as a doctor persuading their patients to adopt healthy habits, is regularly perceived to be harmless. This is true of any social influence that can respect the right of those involved to choose and is not unduly coercive. Alternatively, suppose an individual tries to have his way and uses people against their will. In that case, social influence can be destructive and is commonly looked down upon.

Emotional or psychological manipulation is seen as a form of coercion and persuasion. For the most part, people will see this as abusive or deceptive. Those who decide to employ manipulation will attempt to control the behavior of those around them. The manipulator will have some end goal in mind and will work through various abuse forms to coerce those around them into helping the manipulator get to the final goal. Often emotional blackmail will be involved.

Those who practice manipulation use brainwashing, mind control, or bullying strategies to get other people to finish their duties; the subject may not want to carry out the duties but feel like they have no option because of the blackmail other techniques. Most manipulative people lack suitable caring and sensitivity towards other people; hence, they may not have an issue with their actions. Other Machiavelli may just want to attain their goal and wouldn't be concerned with who has been hurt or bothered along the way. Besides, manipulative individuals are often afraid to get into a healthy relationship because they fear others will not accept them. Someone who has a manipulative personality will often have the inability to be responsible for their problems, behaviors, and life. Since they cannot take responsibility for these issues, the manipulator will use manipulation techniques to get another person to take over the responsibility.

Manipulators can often use the same tactics found in other forms of mind control to get the influence they want over others. One of the most commonly used tactics is known as emotional blackmail. This is where the manipulator will inspire guilt or sympathy in the individuals they try to manipulate. These two emotions are chosen since they are considered the two strongest of all human emotions and are the most likely to drive others to act in the way the manipulator desires. The manipulator will then be capable of taking complete advantage of the victim, using the guilt or sympathy that he has created to force others into assisting them in meeting their targets. Mostly, the manipulator may be capable of creating these emotions; he can also inspire levels of guilt or sympathy that are out of proportion for the ongoing situation. This means that he makes a situation like missing a party to seem like missing an interview or something very significant.

Emotional blackmail is among the techniques used by manipulators. Another tactic that has been successful for many manipulators is using a form of abuse commonly referred to as crazy-making. The tactic is regularly aimed at making the subject manipulated to have some self-doubt; mostly, this self-doubt becomes very strong that some victims may start having feelings of them going crazy. At times, the manipulator will use forms of passive-aggressive actions to cause crazy-making. They might also choose to show support or approval of the subject verbally but then give non-verbal cues that show contradictory meanings. The manipulator often tries to undermine certain behaviors or events while showing his support for that same behavior. Just in case the manipulator is found in the act, he will use denial, rationalization, justification, and the trickery of ill intent to escape the misfortune.

One of the biggest issues with psychological manipulators is that they are never able to find out what other people around them will need, and they may lose the capability to meet or even consider these needs. This does not excuse the behavior they are doing. Still, other people's needs are often not thought of or not prioritized by the manipulator, so they can perform manipulative duties without feeling shame or guilt. This makes it tough to stop the behavior and explain rationally why the manipulator stops. Besides, the manipulator may find it difficult for them to form meaningful and long-lasting friendships and relationships because the people they are with will always feel used and will have difficulty trusting the manipulator. The issue goes both ways of forming relationships; the manipulator may not recognize other people's needs, whereas the other person may not create the required emotional connections or confidence with the manipulator.

Requirements to Successfully Manipulate

A successful manipulator must have tactics at hand that will make them successful at using people to achieve their own final goal. While there are several theories on what makes a manipulator, we will look at the three requirements that have been set out by a successful psychology author known as George K. Simon. According to Simon, the manipulator will need to:

1. Be capable of determining their intended subject's susceptibilities to determine the techniques that will be the most efficient in meeting their objectives.

2. Be capable of concealing their aggressive intentions and behaviors from the subject.

3. Possess some ruthlessness levels that are readily available for them not to deal with any uncertainties that may arise because of harming the victims if it reaches that point. This harm can be either emotional or physical.

The first requirement that the manipulator must accomplish to manipulate his subjects successfully is to conceal their aggressive intentions and behaviors. If the manipulator moves around telling every person his plans or becomes mean to others, then no individual is likely to stick around for long to undergo manipulation. Rather, he needs to be capable of concealing his thoughts from other people and behave as if everything is okay and normal. Often, those who are being manipulated will not realize it, at least not in the beginning. The manipulator will be sweet, act like their best friend, and maybe assist them in solving some issues. By the time the victim becomes aware of the issue, he has had enough knowledge about them to compel the subjects into the proceeding.

Next, the manipulator will need to find out what the susceptibilities of their intended subjects are. This can help them to establish the techniques that need to be used to reach the overall goal. At times the manipulator can do this step through a little bit of observation, while other times, they will need to interact with the subject before coming up with the full plan.

The third requirement is that the manipulator needs to be ruthless. It will not go well if the manipulator puts in all their work and then worries about how the subject is going to fair in the end. If they did care about the subject, they would not likely be going through with this plan at all. The manipulator will not care about the subject at all and does not care if any harm, either physical or emotional, befalls the subject as long as the overall goal is met. One reason manipulators are so successful is that the subject often does not realize that he is being manipulated until later. He may think that everything just fine; he may think that perhaps he has gotten a new friend in the manipulator. The manipulator will use various techniques that may include emotional blackmail to get his way at the end.

CHAPTER 2:

What Is Persuasion?

There are many times when the human mind is pretty easy to influence, but it does take a certain set of skills to get people to stop and listen to you. Not everyone is good with influence and persuasion, though. They can talk all day and would not be able to convince others to do what they want.

On the other hand, some could persuade anyone to do what they want, even if they had just met this person for the first time.

Knowing how to work with these skills will make it easier for you to recognize a manipulator and be better prepared to avoid them if needed. The first thing that we need to look at is what persuasion is. Persuasion is simply the process or action taken by a person or a group of people when they want to cause something to change. This could be about another human being and something that changes their inner mental systems or their external behavior patterns.

Pathos, Ethos. Logos: The Three Emissaries of Public Opinion Modern Day Aristotle

Ethos

This technique portrays the speaker as an ethically qualified expert on the topic in question. In most cases, the speaker has titles that reinforce this idea, such as a professor or master.

This title builds the audience's trust in the speaker.

[20]

The presenter may use the following strategies to convince and persuade the audience.

- Showing unmatched mastery of the topic. This is demonstrated through the use of various terminologies associated with the topic. Some of these terminologies are strange to the audience

- Being introduced by established authorities to speak to the audience. This attaches more importance to the person, thus increasing the amount of respect they command from the audience.

- Their command of language is flawless. The speech is characterized by heavy vocabulary. Their use of grammar and articulation of words leaves the audience in awe. This makes it hard not to listen and heed their words.

- They show a fair-minded approach and analysis of ideas. The presenter shows sincerity to the audience by giving proof and

- Illustrations to give credulity to their ideas. They also attach a lot of logic and reasoning to their speech.

- Sharing a list of their accomplishments with the audience as a way of gaining more credibility. This is mostly accompanied by evidence, such as referring the audience to the internet to search for those achievements.

Combining all these tactics yields tremendous results when it comes to persuading their audience. The effectiveness of this method arises from the ignorance of the audience. The speaker uses this ignorance to manipulate their minds into thinking they are being educated. The presenter's supposedly superior knowledge neutralizes even those who got some insight into the topic.

This technique is used in dark psychology to introduce manipulative concepts into the audience's minds after weakening their reasoning ability.

The example below illustrates the use of the concept of ethos as a persuasion technique in dark psychology.

"As your chief has told you, I am the manager in charge of marketing and recruitment. I understand most of you don't have jobs. I will give you a little story about myself. I started selling herbal medicine when I was still in the first year of university. I couldn't secure a job for over a year after leaving school despite my high grades. Lee introduced me to "Precious Nature Company Int". five years ago, a world-famous enterprise that has given hope to tens of thousands of hopeless souls. I was asked to make an investment of thirty thousand dollars alongside a registration fee of twenty dollars. I didn't earn anything for the first three months, but my earnings started growing from the fourth month. Right now, I earn half a million dollars every month without commissions from the people I have brought to join the company. That Mercedes you see outside is worth fifty thousand dollars, and it was bought with commissions only. I am here to show you how."

We can see all the features of ethos in this short speech. The speaker is persuading his audience to join some pyramid scheme. Not all businesses that operate like this are pyramid schemes, but most pyramid schemes operate this way. The speaker has been introduced by the chief, a figure of authority. The speaker's title is also indicated, a big title for that matter. The speaker shows that he is willing to help them make a fortune just like he did; he even shows them the evidence- a ten-million-dollar Mercedes Benz. Due to the level of respect the speaker commands under his title, accomplishments, and 'knowledge' of the subject, coupled with the audience's desperate situation of joblessness, the audience's probability of doing as the speaker asks is very high.

Logos

This is the use of facts and figures to support the speaker's thesis. The term 'logos' is derived from the word 'logic' which involves the use of reason to give weight to ideas. The presenter may exaggerate these facts and figures as a way of convincing and confusing the audience. Logos also reinforces ethos since the presenter looks more knowledgeable to the audience by simply applying logic in their presentation. In the world of dark psychology, the kind of reasoning used is marred with inaccuracies, falsified or non-contextualized data, outright misrepresentation of facts, and generally misleading information. Logos is a technique of persuasion in dark psychology that has the following features.

- The speaker is more theoretical in their speech. This makes it difficult to ascertain some of their claims, but the target audience believes them anyway. The strategy is meant to keep the audience in the dark until the agent gets whatever they want from them. The agent is afraid of giving practical examples because the probability of tripping over is quite high, which is made worse by the lack of credibility of those ideas.

- Widespread use of abstract language. Their speech is characterized by numerously concealed facts meant to keep the target audience off-balance deliberately. This concealment is achieved through the use of difficult vocabulary that's hard for the audience to understand. The language is simply too technical for the common man. Very few people dare to ask questions on something they have very little understand of in the first place.

- The agent uses wrong or inaccurate definitions most of the time. This works by further misleading the audience about the subject at hand. The speaker will deliberately twist the meaning of some terminologies to align them with their objective. The audience might not object to this deliberate non-contextualization because of the low level of their grasp on the subject. This leaves them vulnerable to persuasion and manipulation.

- Extensive use of citations and quotations; the speaker will refer to experts and authorities' works as a way of reinforcing their persuasion. Dark psychologists would often make their quotations and citations based on imaginary or inaccurate sources.

The following example illustrates the concept of logos concerning dark psychology.

"We have made tremendous steps as a government in ensuring equitable distribution of natural resources. The wells and oil refinery in this region alone have provided jobs to over ten thousand people in the last two years, most of them being youths. At this rate, it means there will be over a hundred thousand jobs created in ten years. We also want to ensure every household has electricity by the end of the following year. Data collected by a renowned American research firm indicates that countries that have reached this power provision milestone have a life expectancy above 80 years. Think of it like this, the retirement age in this country is sixty years. With a life expectancy of eighty years, it means you have around twenty years left in your pocket to enjoy the retirement benefits and watch your children grow. But what happens when you die early? There is something called psychological trauma, which is the brain's inability to grow and think properly due to a sad event. This is what your loved ones will undergo when you leave them that early. As you may be aware, 10 percent of all deaths worldwide are a result of psychological trauma. Let us help the government meet these goals by paying our taxes generously. What is an addition of 5 percent compared to the many benefits that come with it?"

This government official tries to persuade people to pay an additional 5 percent in taxes to support government projects. There are many flows in this speech that only point at some mischief. The area is endowed with a natural resource that is even refined there, but it is still marginalized; residents don't have access to electricity. The speaker presents unverifiable information and crooked reasoning where the promise of a better future is based on his assumptions and is also tied to acceptance of extra tax the government wants. The residents might be persuaded based on the speaker's use of 'logic' to lure them and not because it is the right thing to do.

Pathos

This is a persuasion method where the presenter uses the audience's emotional appeal to advance their agenda. This technique invokes strong feelings and emotions among the audience. It is designed to make the target act in a certain way as a result of emotional provocation. Dark psychologists have used this technique to drive people into acting impulsively without considering the outcome of their actions. Some of the feelings a presenter invokes in the audience include anger, extreme happiness, pity, and fear. The presence of these feelings reduces the effectiveness of thinking and reasoning by a huge margin. The following features are associated with the device of pathos in the world of dark psychology.

- **Use of a vivid and concrete language**. This is designed to create a visualization of the subject in the audience's minds. The language involves a lot of illustrations and descriptions using objects the audience is most familiar.

- **Emotionally loaded tone and language**. The speaker's kind of language draws pity from the audience; these feelings then generate anger and a fierce reaction. With such charged emotions, the target audience can do almost anything they are asked after that meeting.

- **There is too much figurative language**. The audience is left to relate what the speaker is talking about and uncover the real event. This way, the target audience will have an exaggerated picture of the event or situation. This motivates them to react exactly the way the presenter expected.

- **The lengthy narration of emotional events.** This is meant to reinforce the emotional attachment of the matter by the audience. The longer the narration lasts, the more the emotions run high among the audience, and the faster they will respond.

CHAPTER 3:

The Framework of Dark Psychology

A framework, within all realms of science, is a structured approach consisting of separate sectors that support a theoretical study or research. Within the broad range of popular psychology, there is a theoretical framework consisting of five points and a psychological framework used in general psychiatric practice. Both of these things are applied to Dark Psychology. The theoretical framework is altered very little in dark psychiatric works, while the psychological framework varies with the type of work being performed (treatment or study). The theoretical framework consists of Structure, Function, Behavior, Cognitive Ability, and Psychoanalysis.

Structuralism: This entity of the psychological theoretical framework is implemented every time. The goal is to identify the specific points of the patient's psychological experiences using a technique called introspection. Introspection was developed by psychologist Wilhelm Wundt and relied on the patient's reflection of their internal emotions and thoughts. These thoughts and feelings are then processed into the most basic forms of consciousness.

Functionalism: Functionalism was introduced not long after Wundt's student, Edward B. Titchener, formally released structuralism to the psychological community. Functionalism was inspired by intellectuals and brilliant minds such as Charles Darwin. Functionalism took structuralism and pushed out the idea of focusing on the elements of a person's consciousness and, instead, focused on the individual patient and what differences were accounted for.

Behaviorism: This entity of Psychological frameworks was originally brought forth in 1913 when John B. Watson published "Psychology as the Behaviorist Views It." Behaviorism is completely and solely based on a person's outward actions with no focus given on inner thoughts and emotions. Watson fully encapsulated the idea of behaviorism when he said:

It is believed that all behaviors are due to the conditioning and education a person received from the moment they were born.

Cognitivism: Cognitivism was created as a response to the rise of behaviorism. Psychologists argued that thought was more than a behavior. They believe that thought is what creates behaviors and therefore can't be one on its own. This theoretical practice studies the ideas, thoughts, processes, and intellect and not the individual's behavior.

Psychoanalysis: Psychoanalysis is probably the most widely known framework of traditional psychology. This process involves a bit of each type of above, coupled with childhood experiences and how they relate to the adult process. There is an emphasis on the mental health processes that individuals go through without even knowing they are.

General Psychological Framework

While all of the above are used in some theoretical fashion or another within psychology, the general framework is more in tune with the specific type of treatment that the patient will undergo. There are four main types.

- Psychotherapy within the Humanistic Model

- Psychotherapy within the Cognitive Model

- Psychotherapy within the Psychodynamic Model

- Psychotherapy within the Family Model

All four of these you will find within the mainstream psychological community. However, when you begin to cross over to Dark Psychology, these things change, and the therapy is less and the research more. It will often take a very specific sector of psychology to dive into the minds of someone blocked by Dark Psychology. There are no real explanations as to why these people tend to be more difficult to talk to. Still, those in the .01 percent rarely react to any of the above therapies.

The Dark Continuum

As we mentioned earlier in the book, Dark Psychology is believed to be held on a spectrum that humanity can fit on. All individuals can tap into their dark psyche, but most do only on a minuscule level. Then there are those criminals who move down the spectrum further until the end is made up of that .01 percent of heinous and indescribable crimes.

Imagine that the aspects of Dark Psychology sit on a line. Those that use actions that fall under the dark spectrum sit on this line, all deviance acts of malice, manipulative actions, and perverse behaviors sit somewhere in the dark line. The dark line is not just specific to action but to feelings, thoughts, ideas, and points of view as well. This line represents all dark psyches within the realm of this sector of dark psychology.

In comparison, you can also picture a Venn diagram where the three circles overlap each other. Within each of the sections of the diagram are the thoughts, actions, etc. Some overlap with each other, while others stand alone. The outer edges of the circle can be interpreted as the less volatile sectors of Dark Psychology. In contrast, those intersecting inner circles include, up to, the .01 percent.

While the acts and thoughts within a dark psyche fall into the diagram or line depending on their severity, the Continuum is not meant to be a tool used to decide the specific severity of the occurrence. Nuccitelli is currently working further on this concept as it is not complete. Through more research and a more open expansion of studies within Dark Psychology, the Dark Continuum will filter down to a more precise theory.

The Dark Factor

While relatively new in the world of psychology, the Dark Factor is not something that has been hidden from psychological practice throughout the years. Charles Spearman, an English psychologist, in 1904, made two of the most important discoveries in Psychology to date. The first discovery was based on the idea that there was a general factor of intelligence, the g-factor. This factor defined the rate of scoring for intelligence and found that regardless of the indicator, as long as the test is thorough and sufficient, you will be able to measure a person's cognitive intelligence.

From this theory, over a hundred years later, in 2018, Morten Moshagen, Benjamin Hilbig, and Ingo Zettler published a paper in the Psychological Review, showing their findings on what has been coined the D-Factor. The D-Factor is the Dark Factor of Personality. In simple form, this finding says that by comparing all personality traits of a person, you will find the level in which they fall into the Dark Spectrum. If you can imagine a flower, all the petals represent different personality traits, including those within the dark psyche. The closer to the center a person gets to the level of their traits, the darker the personality is. In the center of that flower is the "D."

In simpler terms, the D represents the level in which a person tends to pursue their interests, despite injury or harm to other people, with the distinct and clear justification of their actions prevalent in their minds. Sometimes, these people may not even believe that the harm done to others is a negative consequence of their actions. Those deep in the D spectrum find their justifications outweigh all safety to other people and pursue their agenda in a negative and harmful manner.

Ultimately, Moshagen and his associates have answered the long-standing question of whether there was one force that unified all dark traits. This would be the D-Factor. It shows that there is not just one single trait that defines a dark psyche. Instead, there is a multitude of human traits, some good and some bad, that culminate into the level of darkness your psyche consists of. The traits used were:

• Spitefulness

• Self-interest

• Sadism

• Psychopathy

• Psychological Entitlement

• Narcissism

• Moral Disengagement

• Machiavellianism

• Egoism

People from all walks of life were tested, and the results were combined and studied. In the end, the team came up with the following conclusions:

It was found that there was a positive relationship between all of the dark traits tested for.

The most relatable D-Factor items fell into patterns that gave a basis for their theory. The theory closely attached the ideas of utility maximization, inflicting disutility, and justifying malevolent beliefs.

They found that the people having higher D-Factor scores, when given money, were more likely to keep it to themselves. On top of this finding, these people were also more likely to have unethical behaviors like cheating.

The D-Factor was closely related to self-centeredness, dominance, impulsive behaviors, a need for power, aggressive tendencies, and morality issues. At the same time, they were also related to sincere actions, fair ideas, avoidance of greed, and modest behavior.

The D-Factor does not relate to only one measure. Even when tested repeatedly, removing different variables from the experiment, the correlations were the same.

The Dark Factor tests were much more complex than just the above tests. Information about the person's background, family history, temperament, and life experiences were also taken into account. This test has paved the way for much further research into the dark temperament. It has been widely accepted amongst the psychological community. This test should lead the idea of Dark Psychology further into the realm of everyday psychology. One question that is often asked, though, is what is at the center of the D-Factor. What type of person is the very darkest, the very center of the flower bud?

This idea is referred to as the Dark Singularity.

The Dark Singularity

Before we dive into the very meaning of Dark Singularity within the realm of Dark Psychology, it is important to note a couple of ideas that will help you further understand the depth that humans can reach with the Dark Factor. While on the surface of everyday life, we tend to think of negative things as having boundaries or borders. Our human brains do not like the idea of something being far more evil or ominous than we are capable of comprehending. Science has a lot of different ideas that the human brain cannot fully wrap itself around.

Singularity in General Terms

In science, a singularity is a point in space and time that has an infinite value. It most often discourses when it comes to the infinite density at the tiny center of a black hole. In theory, the center of a black hole never ends, it is infinite. Therefore, it is theorized that the force of gravity can compress an object so far that it just about has zero volume and becomes infinitely dense. At this point, the point of singularity is believed that space and time no longer exist on the scale that the human mind recognizes. Because space and time are completely different, the laws of physics cannot be applied.

CHAPTER 4:

Covert Emotional Manipulation (Cases)

Covert emotional manipulation is used by people who want to gain power or control over you by deploying tactics that are both deceptive and underhanded. Such people want to change the way you think and behave without realizing what they are doing. In other words, they use techniques that can alter your perceptions in such a way that you think that you are doing it out of your own free will. Covert emotional manipulation is "covert" because it works without you being consciously aware of that fact. People who are good at deploying such techniques can get you to do their bidding without your knowledge; they can hold you "psychologically captive."

When skilled manipulators set their sights on you, they can get you to grant them power over your emotional well-being and even your self-worth. They will put you under their spell without you even realizing it. They will win your trust, and you will start attaching value to what they think of you.

Covert emotional manipulation is more common than you might think. Since it's subtle, people are rarely aware that it's happening to them. In some cases, they may never even notice. Only keen outside observers may be able to tell when this form of manipulation is going on.

You might know someone who used to be fun and friendly. He/She got into a relationship with someone else. A few years down the line, she seems to have a completely different personality. If it's an old friend, you might not even recognize the person she has become. That is how powerful covert emotional manipulation can be. It can

[36]

completely overhaul someone's personality without them even realizing it. The manipulator will chip away at you little by little. You will accept minute changes that fly under the radar until the old a different version of you replaces you, build to be subservient to the manipulator.

Covert emotional manipulation works like a slow-moving coup. It requires you to make small progressive concessions to the person that is trying to manipulate you. In other words, you let go of tiny aspects of your identity to accommodate the manipulative person, so it never registers in your mind that there is something bigger at play.

When the manipulative person pushes you to change in small ways, you will comply because you don't want to "sweat the small stuff." However, there is a domino effect that occurs as you start conceding to the manipulative person. You will be more comfortable making subsequent concessions, and your personality will be erased and replaced in a cumulative progression.

Covert emotional manipulation occurs to some extent in all social dynamics. Let's look at how it plays out in romantic relationships, in friendships, and at work.

Emotional Manipulation in Relationships

There is a lot of emotional manipulation in romantic relationships, and it's not always malicious. For example, women try to modify men's behavior to make them more "housebroken"; that is just normal. However, certain instances of manipulation where the person's intention is malicious, and he/she is motivated by a need to control or dominate over the other person.

Positive reinforcement is perhaps the most used covert manipulation technique in romantic relationships. Your partner can get you to do what he wants by praising you, flattering you, giving you attention, offering your gifts, and acting affectionately.

Even the seemingly nice things in relationships can turn out to be covert manipulation tools and props. For instance, your girlfriend could use intense sex as a weapon to reinforce a certain kind of behavior in you. Similarly, men can use charm, appreciation, or gifts to reinforce certain behaviors in the women they are dating.

Some sophisticated manipulators use what psychologists call "intermittent positive reinforcement" to gain control over their partners. After a random interval of time, he will again go back to the intense positive reinforcement. When the victim gets used to the special treatment, it's taken away. When she gets used to normal treatment, the special treatment is brought back, and it all seems arbitrary. Now, the victim will get to a place where she becomes "addicted" to the special treatment. Still, she has no idea how to get it. Hence, she starts doing whatever the perpetrator wants, hoping that one of the things she does will bring back the intense positive reinforcement. In other words, she effectively becomes subservient to the perpetrator.

Negative reinforcement techniques are also used in relationships to manipulate others covertly. For example, partners can withhold sex to compelling the other person to modify their behavior in a specific way. People also use techniques such as the silent treatment and withholding of love and affection.

Some malicious people can create a false sense of intimacy by pretending to open up to you. They could share personal stories and talk about their hopes and fears. When they do this, they create the impression that they trust you, but their intention may be to get you to feel a sense of obligation towards them.

Manipulators also use well-calculated insinuations to get you to react in a certain way at the moment, to modify your behavior in the long run. Such insinuations can be made through words or even actions. In colloquial terms, we call this "dropping a hint." People in relationships are always trying to figure out what the other person wants out of that relationship, so a manipulative person can drop hints to get you to do what they want without ever having to take responsibility for the actions that you take because they can always argue that you misinterpreted what they meant.

Dropping hints isn't always malicious (for example, if your girlfriend wants you to propose, she may leave bridal magazines out on the table). However, malicious insinuations can be very hurtful, and they can chip away at your self-esteem. Your partner can make insinuations to suggest you are gaining weight. You aren't making enough money or suggesting that your cooking skills aren't any good. People use insinuations to get away with "saying without saying," any number of hurtful things that could affect your self-esteem.

Emotional Manipulations in Friendships

Covert emotional manipulation is quite common in friendships and casual relationships. Friendships tend to progress slower than romantic relationships, but that just means that it can take a lot more time for you to figure out if your friends are manipulative. Manipulation in friendships can be confusing because even well-meaning friends can come across as malicious. That's because there is a certain social rivalry between even the closest friends, which explains the concept of "frenemies."

Manipulative friends tend to be passive-aggressive. This is where they manipulate you into doing what they want by involving mutual friends rather than directly coming to you. Passive aggression works as a manipulation technique because it denies you a chance of directly addressing whatever issue your friend is raising. So in a manner of speaking, you lose by default.

For example, if a friend wants you to do her a favor, instead of coming out and asking you, she goes to a mutual friend and suggests that she asks you on her behalf. When a mutual friend approaches you, it becomes very difficult for you to turn down the request because of added social pressure. When you say no, your whole social circle now perceives you as selfish.

Passive aggression can also involve the use of silent treatment to get you to comply with a request. Imagine a situation where one of your friends talks to everyone else but you. It's going to be incredibly awkward for you, and everyone will start prying, wondering what the issue is between the two of you, and taking sides on the matter.

Friends can also covertly manipulate you by using subtle insults. They can give you back-handed compliments that have hidden meanings.

Some friends can manipulate you by going on a "power trip" and controlling your social interactions. For example, there are those friends who insist that every time you hang out, it should be in their apartment or at a social venue of their choosing. Such friends often intend to dominate your friendship, so they are keen to always have the "home ground advantage" over you. They'll try to push you out of your comfort zone just so that you can reveal your weaknesses, and you can then become more emotionally reliant on them.

Manipulative friends tend to excessively capitalize on your friendship, and to a disproportionate degree. They will ask you for lots of favors with no regard for your time or your effort.

Emotional Manipulation at Work

There are many reasons why your colleague may want to manipulate you. It could be you are on the same career path, so he wants to make you look bad. It could be that he is lazy, and he wants to stick you with his responsibilities. It could also be that he is a sadist, and he just wants to see you suffer.

One-way people at work exert their dominance over others is by stressing them out and then, almost immediately, relieving the stress. Say, for example, you make a minor error on a report, and your boss calls you into his office. He makes a big fuss and threatens to fire you, but then towards the end, he switches gears and reassures you that your job is secure as long as you do what he wants. That kind of manipulation works on people because it makes them afraid and gives them a sense of obligation at the same time.

Some colleagues can manipulate you by doing you small favors, and then reminding you of those favors every time they want something from you. For instance, if you made an error at work and a colleague covered for you, he may hold it over your head for months or even years to come. He is going to guilt you into feeling indebted to him.

CHAPTER 5:

Victims of Manipulation

Before we talk about the victims of manipulation, the first thing that might come to your mind is why people manipulate? There can be numerous reasons why people choose the way of manipulation instead of persuasion. The first thing can be that they do not know the difference between them. Second, when people do not have the skills to achieve something in the right manner and feel helpless and hopeless, they start to manipulate people. Also, there is this fear of being left out or being abandoned. Just to gain attention, they think that manipulation can play a good role.

The next reason can be when they want to control and dominate others. They start using their anger, aggression, being extra sweet, etc. They use all the techniques of manipulation to get the work done for you. Another thing can be when they want to raise their self-esteem and lower yours, they use wicked tricks to be in good books of their seniors and want to show that you are weak and less knowledgeable than them.

Manipulators have all the negative thoughts in their minds when they use these techniques as they never do anything to benefit others as they are very self-centered. It is always good to maintain a distance from such people as they are very difficult to handle. If you are in such a situation when people like these cannot be completely avoided, you should always consider your security above everything.

Also, be honest and direct with these sorts of people and ask questions straight away from their expectations from you. Never feel guilty or ashamed of any work you do if it is right as these people find reasons to humiliate you. But the best thing you can do to them is to avoid and ignore them. The other thing about these manipulators is that they know who to make their victims.

Skilled manipulators know very well what to look for to make someone their victim. For them, people who like meeting everyone's needs and like pleasing others are the easiest people to target. They choose them as they are easy to manipulate, victimize, and blame. Also, people who do not say no or do not know how to say no are the other manipulators' other targets as these people would do what they say without any trouble.

Other victims for them are people who have less confidence as those people are very easy to mould and convince, they choose them to get their work done. Also, people who do not know how to speak out, keep their opinion, and fight back are the best prey for them. Manipulators very well know whom they can benefit from and who the people to stay away from are. Anyone can be a victim of manipulation, you or me, sometimes small threats, and at times big too. Being a victim is bad but not giving it back is even worse. You should always have the courage to give it back or walk out when you know that someone is taking undue advantage of you.

Let Us See How You Can Cut the Wings of a Manipulator if You Are the Victim

1) **Analyze your mind**. Manipulation only happens when we let it happen. Yes, there are few things in life that we have no control over, but manipulation is not the one. If you think that someone is trying to play dirty manipulation tricks with you, the first thing you should do is analyze your role in the manipulation process. If you think that yes, you are being manipulated, then you are the one who can stop it there and then. Sometimes you do not feel comfortable facing the situation and saying no straight away; in that case, ensure that

you would not say yes too. You should recognize the ability in yourself to control your reactions and handling the situation.

2) **Know what is important.** Things become complicated, and you get manipulated when you do for others and know what is important for them. So, it is crucial for you first to understand what you want to do and what your aim is. Know what matters to you the most, then only you would be able to say no to others and focus on your path. You would then have a reason to say no to the manipulator as a no without reason would give the manipulator a chance to question you.

3) **Ask for transparency.** It is very clear to all of us that manipulators play games, so they are excellent at selling their point of view and getting their work done. But you should also act smartly and always ask how you would benefit from that. If they are wrong, you would judge that by seeing their reactions, and they might even fumble. As they might not be expecting that you would ask, they are not prepared for the answer. The reason behind it is that manipulators always think about themselves and are not concerned about your interest in it. When you start asking questions about your interest, they would understand that you cannot be their victim anymore and would change their target.

4) **Stay adamant.** There are times when it might be very strenuous for you to come out of the control of the skilled manipulators as they are very good at controlling people. They would be charming, manipulative, and determined to let you down and keep you under their control. All these aspects would make it difficult for you to handle them, but you have to be adamant and cut the manipulator's strings by showing them that you are strong and confident and can very well understand their dirty tricks.

These were the few tips to take out manipulators from your life and identify people who are creating a mess in our lives. We can't stand for ourselves until we do not believe in us and start loving ourselves. Firstly, you don't know that you are capable and strong, and others cannot fool you in any way. So just stay true to your values and always vow to do better in your life. When you become a victim of a manipulator, be it your partner, friend, colleague, or boss, it hurts at times, and there might be some adverse effects on you from it. Your mind gets disturbed as things you have not thought of might happen. Emotional manipulation can also lead to trust, intimacy, security, belief, trust, and many other issues like this, which may have more short- and long-term effects on you. The scars of them might not be physically seen but stay within you sometimes for even a lifetime. Let us know some of the effects of manipulation on the victims.

Short Term Effects

- **Avoid eye contact**: Because of a lack of confidence and low-esteem, the victims start to avoid eye contact with people. Victims start feeling small from inside and feel insecure that they do not become a victim for some other manipulator, so they try to avoid eye contact and conversation with people.

- **Cautious and anxious**: They get so broken from inside that to avoid any sort of manipulation in the future, they become extra cautious towards themselves and others both. Victims become too much careful and watchful about others' behavior and start doubting them, which even makes it difficult for them to make friends. They are also anxious all the time just thinking whom to trust and whom to not.

- **Confused**: They also get into a state of shock, thinking that a person who was so dear to them can change and manipulate them like this. They stay confused and in deep thought, just analyzing what and how it happened. Victims sometimes even cannot believe and are confused that this can happen to them; this can be both a long term and short-term effect.

- **Guilt**: Victims might also feel hateful about themselves and guilty about why they did not get to know about them before. Why were they not able to recognize the manipulators and let them take you for granted? Questions might arise in your mind, but you have to be strong and trust yourself. So do not blame yourself as they are skilled manipulators and they are well aware of your weaknesses and how to take advantage of it.

- **Be overcautious**: As they have faced so much in the past, they become extra cautious while talking to others so that the other person does not get upset or angry about anything you do. This behavior of the victims makes them think a lot which makes them anxious and too much stressed.

- **Self-questioning**: You start questioning yourself about the past things and whatever you do in the present too. You try to think if you recall everything the same way it happened or not. This happens because manipulators question you for each and everything you do or at times also make you realize that you do not remember things right. So, in every situation, you meet with the feeling of doubt about yourself, but you need to trust in yourself and move on.

Long-Term Effects

- **Feeling hateful**: You might feel irritated, impatient, and frustrated. All these factors inculcate within you after being manipulated. When someone treats you negatively, it becomes tough to take it out of your mind. You start feeling resentful and hating others too.

- **Depressed**: You start feeling depressed, especially when you have been emotionally manipulated. You have been told so many lies that your trust breaks to such an extent that you start feeling depressed, and it seems difficult for you to come out of it. But you do not need to worry, it may be a long-term effect, but it can be healed with time.

- **Feeling numb:** You feel like staying alone and would stop reacting to things. This numbness is very dangerous, and you should always try to stay with your friends or loved ones in this situation. Even in situations that make you happy and content, you would not feel good and want to move out of it. You would feel hopeless and broken but do not let one incident become you a victim for a lifetime. Just stay with your close ones and try to cope with the situation by reading positive books and watching movies or listening to music does anything that makes you feel good.

- **Too much observant**: After being the victim, you start observing and judging things excessively, you may just think of everyone in the same way and judge them accordingly. They would not even try to control you, but you would always feel that they want to control you or want to benefit from you, but this is not the truth. For this, you would have to let the past go. Yes, you have to be careful, but at least give yourself one more chance.

CHAPTER 6:

How to Recognize if Someone is Manipulating You

Are you a reliable, conscious, loyal, and honest person?

I'm sorry for you, but then you are the favorite victim of manipulators. Manipulators are always looking for this type of people precisely because they can easily manipulate and do not find much difficulty. That is because the manipulative person completely lacks empathy and morality. So he doesn't care in the least to abuse your kindness and good character. It's just easier for them to attack. By now, these types of people can, unfortunately, be found in any social class and any environment.

Over the years, manipulators have spread to any field. We can find it at the top of a multinational company, as well as in every family's father. Remember, thinking that people are polite to you due to your kindness is not the smartest idea. You are not realistic if you think that. You are thinking overly positive. In most cases, where you find yourself doing a favor to a person, they will not reciprocate.

In most cases, he will speak badly about you. That is because the human being is made like this, and even more so are the manipulators. They will go to great lengths to take any energy you have and then pass it on to another person. As we have seen above, manipulators use countless techniques to enslave us. This involves a very important fact. Watch out for people you have a lot of trust with.

Most of the time, we can indeed find manipulators at work or in any case in those fields, but we often have them at home and do not notice anything. Within families, there are sometimes great manipulators.

Once, it happened to a great friend of mine. He had had a family business for several years. He was working in the field of carpentry. His father and uncle worked within the company. I had always realized that my uncle was a rather strange person from the outside, and I told him so many times. He didn't listen to me. He always replied that they knew each other well and that they were very close to have no problems. I broke off the conversation by seeing his belief in what he was saying, but I wasn't at all sure it was the truth. One day he writes to me to meet to have a coffee. I knew immediately from his tone that something was wrong and I ran to his house. Guess what happened? The uncle had long ago manipulated them to make them open accounts between them and all banking things visible. One day, his uncle had disappeared along with all the carpentry shop's savings; $ 200,000 disappeared into thin air. He heard nothing more about his uncle. Be aware of all situations that seem safe and trustable to you because those are the most dangerous ones. No expert manipulator stands out while doing it. Of course, I'm not telling you to be afraid of your family or friends. They are not all manipulators or predators.However, all the victims of manipulation are unaware of the situation. This is the real problem to be solved. Thus, it is right to know all the manipulation techniques, so we notice once they are used on us. This way, we will be ready to realize we are in a manipulative situation.

CHAPTER 7:

Manipulation in a Relationship and at Work

The culture romanticizes deceptive relations so much when talking about a love that it can be hard to recognize them for what they are. We have lots of literature suggesting that genuine relationships are about fixation, that pure love is all-out, and that infatuated people have no boundaries or separate lives.

While many people romanticize the concept of a deceptive relationship, we have to realize that it is not real love. Sometimes it may trigger a dramatic storyline and tension that keeps the reader engaged. Still, there is no fun living through a deceptive relationship that is romantic.

You may have been warned of manipulating people and the fact that coercion and mistreatment are worrying; the facts are that being in a relationship of control and manipulation that never develops into ill-treatment can also be terrifying and dangerous. Just because somebody does not harm you physically does not mean you cannot feel pain from their actions yet.

Being dominated or put down by a partner can damage our faith, make us feel fearful of relationships in the future, and leave us feeling lost rather than comforted, with various mental and emotional injuries with which we should not be burdened.

You may be familiar with the symptoms of a negative relationship. You might have met a partner, for instance, who required you to wear only certain clothing items or did not want you to visit your friends and family.

This person might want to know where you are going, what you are doing, and why you are just a couple of minutes late. Manipulators are frequently very anxious people, allowing nervous thoughts to pass through their brains and control their actions. We channel their intense fear and anxiety into hallucinations about what you might do if you are not around them. They will think about their worst fears and what you can do to damage them, so they will assume you are doing these things when you are not around.

Such things may spur them to hate you if you are not around. Sometimes it may seem flattering to have someone so concerned about you. You might think, "It is so sweet that they always want to know where I am, and I am safe," but it is not their intention when someone is going to take great steps to control you.

Unfortunately, they are not concerned about your well-being. Therefore, the manipulators are thinking, "I need to make sure I know where this person is at all times, so they do not do something that I do not approve of." Your presence is their assurance that you are not meeting their worst fears about the bad things that you are doing to them when you are not both of you together. In this case, they will not be addressing your needs. The manipulator behaves only to serve the interests of his own.

A manipulator will never tell you that but will only be worried about improving how they look to you. They are always going to use this technique to make sure you feel guilty. They will make you feel guilty if you do not respond for 20 minutes, instead of admitting that it is acceptable for a person not always to write back immediately. They would view you as if you did something wrong or disrespectful to them because, at the time, you were not around your phone or too busy to answer first.

Marriage should feel better, not confining, scary, or distressing, and having an accomplice will make you happier, not more sorrowful.

There will be hard times in life. Your mate may not be understood, and they may not understand you. On the way to making you stronger, these challenges should be pure obstacles. There shouldn't be a healthy relationship that continuously drains you and tears you down, making you feel constantly exhausted.

Signs of a Manipulative Relationship

Most of us have had terrible things happening in our lives— enough terrible things that the prospect of a hero sweeping us off our feet and protecting us from any problems for whatever remains of our lives can sound extremely tempting. For this reason, we are sometimes looking in the wrong places for security, empathy, and care.

Reconsider whether your partner's support thoughts include stopping you from making your own decisions and living your own life. A partner who secures you by assuming responsibility for your maxed-out accounts, or perhaps speaking to a partner you have been struggling with, does not pay special attention to you; they are trying to make you have no choice but to put all your faith in them and no one else.

A true partner knows they cannot protect you and what it holds from everyday life — they can just support you when you need them. Run into a money-related issue at some point. A trusted partner can help you pray an overabundance of unopened bills— give help, but do not take control of the situation. They will not take your passwords or insist that only a small amount of money per month be allowed until you have paid off all of your current debt. A true partner is going to offer help yet realize you need to manage your problems.

One common manipulative relationship is making us feel guilty when we see friends and family members. If we imagine someone trying to cut off their partner from their emotionally supportive network, we envision something similar to the contemptible husband in a movie made for TV that threatens his better half that she will never talk to her closest friend again. Nevertheless, deceptive spouses can also inconspicuously isolate you from your support network.

A shrewdly manipulative person will not outwardly discourage you from seeing your family because it can be an obvious sign that you should be running in the opposite direction. We will make the coercion more subtle, rather than slowly dragging you out of your life, rather than an outright ban. If your partner can convince you to apologize for an action that you know you have not done wrongly and that you are doing, your manipulative partner will realize that he or she can force you to do whatever they want you to do.

Each time you go out with your buddies, your partner can sulk until you blow off other friends just to save the tension. Perhaps your partner will make negative remarks about your loved ones until you begin to believe that the thoughts they have about these people are valid.

You may even have a hobby or an event you enjoy trying to get your manipulator to stop doing it. They will ensure that you know that your interest is idiotic and will ridicule you until you give it up.

The scrutiny of a controlling partner may not always appear as such. It can be framed reasonably and rationally, implying that your partner is just trying to help you. They might even tell you they are trying to help you.

At school, they will research your decisions. Some of their sentences may include: "Why do you choose to use it for your presentation? You are not thinking about what the boss will think? They are going to question your spending habits and how you are going to buy things with questions like, "Did you have to buy another shirt?" Manipulators will spin their words, so it is not clear that the choices you make are wrong, but a seed of doubt and insecurity is being planted.

All partners, however, examine each other periodically. Our loved ones are still supposed to look for us, and sometimes we need others to help us make choices or point out bad habits. Remember, always test this person's true purpose and determine why they had wanted you to change your actions.

Sometimes a manipulator may ask for access to your personal belongings in a relationship. Still, they will not grant you the same rights. We may know all your secrets, but we rarely trust you.

They are not just less likely to share, and they are not helping you.

This type of behavior demonstrates that the other person dominates. Your partner does not reserve the right to search your emails or texts or asking for your passwords because they say they are concerned that you may be cheating. There is a distinction between having insider facts and having healthy independence from your partner, and when you are in a relationship with someone, you do not have to surrender that.

Every so often, sincere couples healing from a disaster would require the weakened spouse to view the messages of each other as a form of transparency. But, if this is not an agreement you have worked out directly with your partner, it is incorrect.

By emotional influence, coercion is all about influencing the way someone else thinks and acts. Coercion is veiled with emotion, or at least what appears to be a sort of empathy. Most of the time, this is a calculated attempt by the manipulator concerned to relate to the victim.

We must recognize the impact it has had on us to overcome this manipulation completely. If you want a healthy relationship with someone, we must look at all the ways we have been affected by their relationship. It may be the first sign that there is a manipulative relationship if that impact is negative.

- Most manipulative people have four standard attributes: they know the weaknesses.

- They use your vulnerabilities against you.

- They persuade you to surrender something of yourself to serve them through their quick plots.

- If a controller triumphs in manipulating you, he will likely repeat the crime until the mistreatment is stopped.

They are going to have a lot of different reasons for keeping you around and controlling you. One might just be because a past relationship damages them. We may have confidence issues that have made it difficult for them to be transparent and consider other partners. This situation can make them feel like they need to manipulate you to keep you loyal to them.

Many partners could be lonely people who are desperate for love and attention. You will stop at nothing to make sure you stick around, even if that means bribery, whether you feel like you will take that path or are afraid you will abandon them.

You may also just want practical things from you, such as financial support, your shared house, a car, and other benefits that are not connected to you as a person they love, but rather the life you choose to live. These are some of the most dangerous manipulators and are as normal as the others.

CHAPTER 8:

Differences Between Manipulation and Persuasion

Truly, these two concepts are very closely related, and most people get confused between their differences and meanings, and the line between them seems blurred. You must figure out when you are crossing the line of persuasion and entering into the manipulation zone. Hence, before understanding the difference in them, let us first understand their meaning, which would automatically clear out the difference.

Persuasion means when you say or act so that people do or believe what you are saying. Persuasion is something that we do every day daily. Persuasion is never taken in an evil or negative way. We can say that it is the way we interact with the people who are around us. At times while discussing any topic, when we try to keep our point and prove ourselves right, that is also persuasion. It also comes into the picture when you want someone to do something right and want to see this world as a better place. Also, you try to persuade people when you want to earn a profit or sell a product. Doing this is not being wicked or doing something immoral.

Now, let us understand what manipulation means. It means the act to change by unfair or artful means to serve your purpose. In manipulation, you are not bothered about the other person's benefit, or less what you want to see is your revenue and benefit. In this case, you want your profit no matter what, by any means. If the buyer is also benefiting, then that is good, but they are not concerned about that. Manipulation always comprises the deception and misrepresentation of the product or truth, but it does not go a long way.

[56]

Let us understand this as well by taking an example in relevance to the one mentioned above. Here the company thinks of only their profit while making the profit irrespective of customer needs and requirements. In such cases, the customer would only try the product once, and when they realize that it is not helping them or have been deceived, they will stop buying the product.

Most of the researchers say that the difference between the two comes down to three things, which are:

a) The intention behind your persuasion

b) Transparency and truthfulness behind your desire

c) A benefit to the other person

- These were the major differences between persuasion and manipulation. Yes, there is a very thin line of intention between them, but you need to realize it. Persuasion is always positive, and manipulations are said to be negative and evil. With the help of persuasion in an argument, you try to make the interlocutor adopt your perspective. On the other hand, in manipulation, you bent the truth to get approval from the interlocutor. In persuasion, the opponent willingly accepts your point, but the person is coerced to agree in manipulation.

- Persuasion is usually done to do good things. Here you would recommend the buyer with the best services, try to make the perfect match, and strive to stop using anything harmful. On the contrary, in manipulation, only one of the parties is benefited.

- In persuasion, you present all the right arguments in the best manner, which are logical and convincing both but in manipulation, people try to mould the truth so that they can achieve their selfish goals

- Although, in persuasion, you try to convince others when they do not agree with your point. But the thing is that you are transparent, and the intentions are good and real. On the other hand, manipulation is opposite.

- In persuasion, if the other person agrees to what you were trying to tell, they would benefit from it as it was in their favor. But in manipulation, the other person would regret it after agreeing to your point. The reason behind it is that the truth was not told; the customer had no benefit as the intent was never good.

I am sure that it must be very clear to you what both these things mean and the major differences in them. Therefore, you should always think while convincing someone who does it to benefit just you or the other person. It will become easy for you to understand whether you are doing something wrong or you are right.

Don't you think persuasion is a really good technique and every one of us should imply it in our lives and think about ours and others' benefits too? So, let us learn a few persuasion tactics which would help you in changing other's mind:

- **Scarcity Technique:** This is the most used persuasion technique, and mostly the salesman and marketers use it. I am sure that you must have seen that the product is less in supply; people tend to ask more of it. Thus, if you want to increase your product or service demand, always show that it is available for a limited time. The offer is just for the time being; it would increase the chances of an increase in your product sales. You must have read these lines often, such as never to be seen again, once a year, attaching a timer, limited offer, etc. Also, an experiment was done where one group was given a product which was in great amount, and the other group was given a scarce product. The end of this experiment was the second group could sell more products as people were keen to buy it because it was limited. You as well can use this tactic to increase the demand for your commodities.

- **Social Authentication**: People usually consider this technique as it does not take time to notice that in social groups, people usually there are group thinkers of higher levels. Whenever anyone thinks of a unique idea, whatever everyone agrees or not, but yes, they think and give their point of view. So, whenever you take any decision, in that regard, you will always consider the points that your mates or friends mentioned. For example, many people just start smoking either because it is social proof or their friends, so they also start doing it.

- **Reciprocation**: Most people like returning favors if someone does something good for them. Also, majorly people do not even know that they would like the gift or not; they are just inclined to return the favor. If you make someone feel indebted, that is a good way increases the probability of getting what you desire. For example, you want to collect money for some old age people to get a house. Instead of directly asking for money, according to their talent, you can ask them to make beautiful frames, pots, etc. Give them to people, make them feel indebted, and then ask for a donation. Also, a study was done and seen the more kind the waiter was to the customers, the more tip he got. So, be generous to all, and they would, in turn, return generosity towards you.

- **Authority:** If you want to convince people always to show yourself as a source of authority. Most people look up to authority or a leader, be it any field, and get easily convinced when an authoritative person says something. For example, if you read that 9 out of 10 doctors recommend using a specific soap brand, then most people would run after that brand as it has gained an advantage over others. This states that most people follow someone who has authority, at times, even when they are wrong. This technique explains that you always be confident and have your attitude if you want people to follow you or get influenced by what you say or do.

- **Regularity and commitment**: It has been seen that people who show regularity and fulfill the promises then help them influenced others to do more for them. If you fulfill the commitment and do what you said in time, it influences others. It makes them believe that they can count on you and help you in persuasion when you want them to do something for you. For example, instead of writing signup, many websites use the statement like- join me and the second option is No, I am boring. Statements like this convince customers, and it increases their conversion rates.

- **Foot in the door:** This persuasion technique is very interesting, and many people use it. This technique states that whenever you want a favor from someone, ask for a smaller one and then ask for the bigger favor. It means that when you first ask for help, and if the person says yes, they get committed to doing that, and when you ask for the bigger help, it can act as a continuation for the smaller one. For example, if you fail a test and your teacher says no to taking the test again. You should first always ask for feedback so that you can work on it. And then request the teacher whether they can take the test again. This way, the teacher would see that you are keen to learn and improve and not say no.

- **Door in the face:** Well, this technique has been seen in many stores and supermarkets. It is the opposite of the technique mentioned above. In this method, you first ask for big favors and if the person says no, then request and ask if they can do something easy and small for you. This way, the other person gets convinced and thinks that if not a big help, but yes, they can do a favor by doing something small. For example, you ask your cousin or any mate for Rs.10, 000 if they say no, then you can always say that if not 10,000, can you please help me with Rs. 3000. There are major possibilities that they would say yes.

- **Anchoring:** This is said to one of the most powerful persuasion methods. It has numerous uses but is mostly used in pricing. This technique can be best explained with the help of an example. You go to the market to buy a refrigerator for yourself, the salesman says Rs. 30,999 but you bargain and gets the cost lowered to Rs.27,500. You would be happy that you got a great deal and feel satisfied, instead of knowing that the actual price of it was maybe less than that. But you are happy as, according to you, it was the best deal.

CHAPTER 9:
Methods of Persuasion

For some people, the art of persuasion comes easily. You can watch them talk to almost anyone, and it seems like they will always get the response they want from the other person. On the other hand, some people may have the best massage in the world who couldn't convince anyone, even their closest friends, to do something. No matter where you fall in either of these groups, though, with a little bit of practice and hard work, you will be able to learn how to use persuasion to your advantage.

In terms of the process of using persuasion, there will usually be three parts that you need to follow, including:

- The communicator, or the medium used as the source of persuasion

- The persuasive nature of the appeal

- The audience or the target person that the appeal is going to be sent to.

Each of these elements needs to be accounted for before trying to use persuasion on a higher level. It is always a good practice to look around you and check to see how many persuasion instances are going on in your daily life.

Some of these will be overt, but many of them are going to be pretty subtle. This can be great training for persuasion because you will employ the same kind of tactics.

Using the Aristotelian Appeals

So, the first option that we are going to look at is the Aristotelian appeals. Aristotle is well-known and is one of the most famous persuaders of all time. He believed that there were three main ways that a person could approach the thing when they were trying to use persuasion to change the opinion of the other person.

The first appeal that one could use was ethos, which will focus on things such as trust, integrity, and character. The second appeal that you should work on is pathos, which is when you evoke the other person's emotions. And the third appeal that you can use when it comes to persuasion is logos. This is when you will use logic, rational explanations, and even evidence to help support your claims.

Foot in the Door

This allows you to ask for a bigger favor after you have already been granted a smaller favor, especially if they are related somehow. You may start with something pretty small, such as just borrowing a cup of sugar from your neighbor. Your neighbor will probably be fine with this because it's not that big of a deal, and most people, as long as they have it on hand, will have a cup of sugar to share with you.

This method can be used in many different persuasion circumstances. The trick is to always start with something small, something you think the target will be willing to help you out with. Then you will slowly build yourself up until you get to the bigger thing that you would like them to have in the long run. You may have wanted the target to start with the bigger thing, but you would have completely missed out on the sale if you went there first.

Reversal Tagging

Another option that you can use is known as reversal tagging. This trick uses simple and subtle sentence phrasing to get an agreement, or at least compliance, from the target in general. It will use two opposing structures inside the sentence, the first part is an affirmative statement, and the second one will be a tag question.

This method's key is to ensure that the first statement is pretty strong because it will be the main persuasive component. This technique is also useful when convincing the other person to take action on something, rather than just agreeing with you. It is the same principle, but this time you will state your negative first before taking a long pause and then adding the tag question.

Reverse Ppsychology

You have probably heard about this in the past because it is a psychological tactic that is often used when you want to get the other person to take action. However, if you are not good at performing this tactic, it will seem pretty obvious, and it will not work the way you would like it to. This tactic will get somebody to do what you would like by suggesting that they do the opposite in the beginning. It will be the most effective if you can evoke an emotional response because it will stop the person from thinking rationally through their decision.

Cognitive Dissonance

Have you ever been in a situation where you know that something seems a bit off about it, but you cannot figure out why it doesn't feel right? When there isn't something quite right about a situation, it will set off some dissonance in mind and trigger the person to try to make it all right. People who have OCD will often know this feeling because they will notice when little things are out of the normal.

If you can change things up a little bit, you may convince the other person to act in the way you would like. They may feel that their reputation is falling a little bit, missing out on something, or so much else. You can then step in to offer them a solution, an easy way to change things back to normal, and they are more likely to jump right at it.

Counter-Attitudinal Advocacy

It is pretty common for people to state a view on something or even support an opinion, even if that is not something they believe. This isn't necessarily that deceptive because people choose to do this with is usually small or have the best intentions. When this happens, we attempt to reduce the dissonance that we caused by saying that our actions are still noble.

Whether you think that telling a little white lie or doing something similar is acceptable or that you think honesty is the best option is irrelevant because you can still use this human tendency to your advantage when you are persuading others. This is a common technique to use when it comes to cults or even gangs when trying to change others' beliefs to justify their behavior.

Hurt and Rescue Principle

This principle will be based on evoking some discomfort or fear in the person from the start. When the person is assessing their options for a solution, you will offer the perfect solution in the form of the thing you want to persuade them to. You need to manufacture a level of discomfort here first, and being crafty enough to make this work can be hard. Since you are trying to bring in some fear or discomfort with your target, you need to be careful with this option. It is not a good idea to come off as aggressive or intimidating in the process because this will just turn the person away from you completely.

Auction Model

This strategy is a good one to put in place if you are working with more than one buyer at the same time. Otherwise, it is not going to be the best one. With this method, you want to play one of the parties against the others so that there is a buying frenzy, and it is more likely that the price will be driven up, no matter what you are trying to sell.

It is human nature to be competitive. When faced with some opposition to something they would like, their primitive instincts will come out. Possession seems to be innate for most of us, especially if we haven't rationally appraised the real use of the item ahead of time. The persuader will use their advantage, getting all the buyers in the deal to jump on board and try to pay more than the other person.

As you can see, there are a lot of different techniques that you can use when it comes to being successful with persuasion. The one you will choose often depends on the goals you have in mind, what you are trying to persuade the other person to do, your comfort level, and how hard the other person will be to persuade. Try a few of them out and see which one works the best for you.

CHAPTER 10:

The Basic Principles of Persuasion

The Ability to Persuade Is a Neutral Power

If you want to master the art of persuasion, you need to understand the idea of neutrality. Keep in mind that the rules and capabilities of persuasion are neither good nor evil. Like nuclear technology, which can be utilized to generate electricity or create an atomic bomb, the power to influence others can establish cooperation or force submission. Whether the result is positive or negative depends on the individual using these principles and how he uses them.

Some people want to succeed regardless of the costs. They are willing to use all possible tricks and abuse the principles of persuasion. They often use violence, temptation, blackmail, bribery, and guilts to get what they want.

On the other hand, if used appropriately, persuasion can help promote the growth of an entire community. By using persuasion, we can forge peace agreements between warring countries, initiate fund-raising programs, and convince drivers to follow traffic rules.

Persuasion Requires Adaptation

To become a successful persuader, you can't just imitate what others are doing. You need to have a concrete plan that you can use for the situations you will face. Also, you should not simply memorize all the techniques written in this book. You need to have a clear idea of which specific tools or techniques should be used for any given scenario. To acquire this skill, you need to proactively observe, examine, learn, and apply proper persuasion principles.

Anchoring

This specific technique can be used in a wealth of situations, and it is a powerful way to persuade others once you master it. This technique has you compare two things against one another to persuade someone to agree with you by making them think they are getting the better end of the deal. This is a persuasion technique often used by salespeople.

For example, you go to a car lot, and you see a vehicle priced at $12,000. You talk the salesperson down to $9,500 and think you got a fantastic deal. In reality, the vehicle is valued at $8,000, so the dealership came out ahead. However, since they accepted your negotiating price, you feel the deal was good. The salesperson persuaded you to feel the price you paid was good.

There Must Be an Audience

The art of influencing and convincing other people requires listeners – whether it is a large group or just an individual. This persuasion component can never be changed or neglected, so you must learn how to adjust to your listeners' desires quickly, wants needs, and fears. If you want to make sure that you will succeed, you need to master the science of conducting background research and reading your audience.

It is also important that you know the specific tools and techniques that must be used for any given situation. This is because faulty or inappropriate techniques and tools will just create communication barriers between you and your listeners, which will dramatically reduce your chances of successfully convincing them.

Social Proof

This core persuasion principle is also sometimes referred to as Consensus. Social proof feeds directly from the previous storytelling of Commitment and Consistency. We have told ourselves a story of what we believe we are, what we stand for, and the kind of person we are. To reinforce that story, we look at how other people behave for Social Proof of how people like us should react in a particular situation.

Successful Persuasion Has Long-Lasting Effects

Effective persuasion is great since it offers enduring effects. Still, it entails the detailed study and solid commitment on the speaker's part. You need to devote time and effort to make sure that your statements have a lasting influence.

Although short-term persuasion tactics may seem to be ideal since they require minimal effort, you will be wasting more time and effort in the long run since your listeners will easily forget about your statements.

In the end, you will have to repeat the process of persuading your audience to make them believe what you are saying.

Authority

Once we have decided on the type of person we are, and we've assembled with the kinds of people we believe that identity; the next step is to seek out knowledgeable people to reinforce what we've told ourselves to be true. That's where the idea of Authority takes hold.

Speaking in "We"

Part of being persuasive is to make people feel like they are not alone. When you are working to persuade someone, never use "you" when talking, but always use "we" instead. They will feel that by doing what you ask, they are helping themselves too. It also makes them feel like they are a part of something, which is a big motivating factor when someone will do something they normally would not.

Liking

This weapon will entail the manipulative individual who will be motivated to make the victim like them. This is because once the victim likes this manipulative individual, there is usually more likely to say yes to them if ever they make any request. There are mainly two main factors that will contribute to how well the victim will like his manipulator.

Reciprocity

This weapon is used so that the victim will try to repay the manipulator in kind when the manipulator provides the victim with something of value. This means that when the manipulator performs some kind of service to the victim, they will tend to feel that at some point, they have an obligation to perform a similar service.

While the two services may not be the same, they have the same value to match each other's obligations.

The act of reciprocation ends up giving the subject a sense of obligation, which the manipulator can then use as a powerful tool when they want to use persuasion.

Commitment and Consistency

This is where the manipulative individual will have to use both of these tools if they want any person to change their point of view of any particular thing. They are easier to understand when things are consistent and can help the subject make better decisions. It's not good for the manipulator to always change the facts they use or change other information needed to help the victim process the information.

Scarcity

Speaking of evolution's early days, our final persuasion principle is an obvious holdover from the early days of staying alive. Scarcity makes things more valuable to us, so when something seems like it is limited in quantity, we are more likely to want it.

Survival depends on specific resources that can be in short supply, so humans are naturally prone to try and save and hang on to that which is not always available. Since this is core hardwiring in our brains, we'll see that this is an often-used method of persuasion today.

This is a weapon of influence that many people tend to be a bit familiar with but is often underestimated due to the basic definition of scarcity. If for one reason or another a particular idea or product has a limited time for which is available, it is most likely that a higher price will be attached to it. As human beings, we are usually obsessed with chasing after that which we cannot get.

CHAPTER 11:

Everything That Makes You Vulnerable: How to Protect Yourself

To avoid people who would like to manipulate us, we must know what they specifically look for in their victims. A bit like prey, it should understand how to escape the predator without being caught for any reason.

To do this, you need to do a self-analysis job to understand if you have even just one character trait among those that I will indicate shortly after that.

Many people take it for granted that they are always treated well because it follows the morals and good fellowship that should always be among human beings. But obviously, this is not the case, and it is precisely necessary to understand where we could be attacked. The biggest problem is that these people hide perfectly among those you don't expect.

They are very good at using the sense of trust that a person has to take advantage of them without restraint. We have all seen at least one movie where there is a couple who arrives from a foreign city, and for whatever reason, they meet a couple of neighbors. Initially, everything goes well. They all go out to dinner together, borrow things when they are needed, and so on.

When for a futile cause, everything starts to collapse, and a real hate relationship is born between them, and the chaos begins. Fortunately for us, these relationships are not normal, but nowadays they have increased more and more.

They can also be found in any social class. None excluded.

Consequently, it has become essential to be aware of these topics to be ready when everything explodes and not be immobile to suffer situations.

Now to help you understand if you can be another manipulative person, I am going to list a series of specific characteristics that these people look for in their victims.

It doesn't mean that if you are a weak person and have everything that I will list, you will meet some bad people.

But surely, my dispassionate advice as if we were brothers is to raise your guard.

Always remember that it is wrong, but people take it out on the weakest of them or, rather, those who seem to be less strong.

The Anxiety of Being Accepted

- That is a condition that is very easy to find in people today.

- This condition has spread even more with the advent of social networks.

- Most people's brains are now unbalanced.

- The "Like" button has changed the lives of millions and millions, if not billions of people. Our brain was used to being loaded with dopamine and cortisol from time to time.

- Dopamine is released when our brain undergoes a positive impulse, while cortisol is used by our body when a negative thing happens.

- These two essences that our body releases make us maintain a certain balance with ourselves.

- But to date, the parameters of these have been hit destroyed by social networks. Now everything rounds around that.

- When somebody receives likes, his dopamine level rises. Negative comments instead make cortisol levels going up. Three likes and you get dopamine, dopamine, and dopamine.

- All this due to the complete imbalance of people who are now seeking constant approval from others. Try to weigh it. If you post a photo today and fewer likes arrive, how do you feel?

- Maybe you are different and out of these characteristics, but it's hard to believe, and 99% of the time, if you say that you do not have these problems, you are lying to yourself.

- You feel sad as if someone had abandoned you.

- But nothing serious happened. Indeed, the more detached you are from all these social networks, the better you feel.

- For example, I have deleted all of my social accounts.

- You don't need them.

- Now I'm sure you are thinking about two things. The first is "I could do it, but I don't want to because I spend my time there," the second is "it's too excessive, I spend little time a day."

- In the vast majority of cases, this is not the case, and if you go on the phone in the settings, it tells you exactly how much time you waste on social networks.

- Think that all that time, you are being manipulated. You see a world that doesn't exist. On Instagram, guys all have 6 pack abs, or if you are a girl, the others all have fantastic bodies.

- Then you go to the beach and ask yourself, "but where are the people who are on social media?

- Delete them. You will see how relieved you will feel and start thinking on your own without being manipulated by anyone.

The Fear of Expressing Negative Emotions

- Very often, manipulators are overly attracted to people with this trait.

- Those people are reluctant to show their negative emotions because they do not want to be misjudged by other people.

- The manipulators are just super attracted because they understand that whatever they decide to do to a person with these characteristics, it will be fine, and they will never tell anyone anything.

- It happens many times in love relationships.

- It is hard to see a manipulator looking for such a person at work. While in relationships, it is much more likely that the manipulator is present.

The Inability to Say No

- People with this trait always think that saying no is wrong. If you do that, then you are not a nice person, and they want to be so.

- The main problem is that you should look at your interests first and then those of others. Also because, if a person asks you something, he is thinking of himself. Try to think about it.

- But manipulators are super adept at making the person think they have to stay under and follow everything the other says.

- That often happens in the workplace.

- Where there is the boss who decides, everyone obeys, and no one can say no. In that case, you are undergoing a manipulation that will cause you to remain a slave to that person in the long run.

- It will initially ask you to do this and do that. It starts with small favors until he gets to control you as if he had a magic wand.

Little Self-Sufficiency

- It is precisely the icing on the cake that manipulators are looking for. When people are looking for help, they risk running into a manipulator who will be ready to take advantage of this.

- That is because once the manipulator has helped you, the favor that he will ask you will be ten times greater.

- You must avoid this situation like death. When you need a hand, only go to people who you are sure will help you with nothing in exchange or who will not do it again in the future.

Absence of Self-Direction

- It is very similar to the previous one but has some essential differences. It is not about helping someone who has a problem. Here the person is lost.

- Not in the sense that he has to go to a club and doesn't know which way to take, but he can't understand what he wants from life or what to do in a particular situation in his life.

- Here all the possible manipulators that you can meet come out. I see a great opportunity. A person who has no idea what to do is the best thing that can happen to a manipulator.

- He brings him to do what he wants. It will lead him to make choices just because he manipulated him well.

- People in this situation are like the holy grail of manipulators.

Genuineness

- Perhaps one of the worst conditions is genuineness.

- The manipulators of the sale greatly exploit this condition. They use people's ingenuity to rip them off and steal their money.

- This condition is not always visible in the person, but it often comes out in difficult times. Many victims of manipulators are precisely people in economic difficulties.

- When a manipulator sees that a person is in trouble with money, he uses the latter's feelings to make him trust the manipulator who offers him quick and easy money.

- It is a highly incorrect policy that manipulative people adopt on temporarily weak people.

- I'll give you an example of a weak person momentarily to make it clearer to you.

If someone finds himself in the situation of having to send his child to a college but does not have the money for it, he may find someone, online or in presence, it makes no difference that guarantees him to find the money just by clicking here and there on your computer.

What Do You Think the Person Does?

- It doesn't mean being stupid, and most of the time, people who fall for these tricks know very well that you don't get rich that easily.

- But the skilled manipulator succeeds with a series of sentences that destroy all the security of the manipulated person and, in a short time, brings him to his side.

- This technique is unfair because it plays on the people's feelings, and most of the time, the manipulator takes everything that the person has and destroys his life.

- Manipulators succeed easily, without even putting in too much effort.

No Self-Esteem

- These people are always highly sought after by manipulators for one simple reason. With a few compliments and a few nice words, they manage without any problem to bring the victim to their side.

- Unfortunately, many people have this problem nowadays. The increase in this phenomenon has been amplified by the fact that people seek attention on the internet.

- That creates anxiety and a sense of inadequacy, and the manipulators feed on this situation.

Submissive Personality

People who believe in others don't have to be ashamed or anything like that, but they need to know that they are among the most coveted prey of manipulators.

Many of them approach the person to make them start to think well of them. But after gaining the trust of the person, the manipulator can easily play his game.

Immaturity

- It is another feature highly sought after by manipulators.

- Immature people are overly malleable, and this makes them one of the most desired people.

- This is what happens to all those kids who are manipulated by groups to become part of them. But this leads kids on the wrong track and make them slaves of these people.

- Just a few can get out of the loop because most people will feel addicted to it, which will tie them to the manipulators. The latter will lead them more and more on the bad road for their convenience.

- How many guys have you seen changing in a short time just because of their new friends?

- I imagine many, as I have seen. Of course, friendships change for a million reasons ranging from fights to moving to another country.

- But the most important thing is to understand who you are approaching and see if these people are the ones we want to date without the fear of being alone.

Impressionability

- Manipulators looking for this character can be easily found on the internet. Social networks are full of these people.

- People who flaunt things they don't have or show a false lifestyle only to get impressionable people's attention so that they can be manipulated with ease.

- They mainly sell something to these people and take away the money for a product or service that the person buys to become like the manipulator.

- Of course, none of these methods ultimately work and so in a short time, all will have been in vain.

Narcissism

- It is an unexpected feature, doesn't it? I already see you saying: but how is that possible? Manipulators are narcissists, so how could they go after narcissists like them?

- Well, they do. And for a simple reason.

- As I explained to you earlier, Narcissists always want to be in the center of attention, and manipulators know this well and use it in their favor.

They start to compliment them so that they can get them on their side, and they will take the trust of these people.

Impulsiveness

- Impulsiveness increases the chances of being manipulated.

- That happens for a reason. When a person is impulsive, he does not pay attention to the consequences of his actions. For the manipulators, this is the icing on the cake.

- They play a lot with this aspect of people because they can make the victim do what they want with a minimum of effort.

- Sometimes they manifest this by causing them to explode. They harm the victim or tell him words that they know affect that person because at that moment, they maybe want them to go crazy

- Or maybe they do the opposite.

- They calm the victim and make them feel good because they may know that this will benefit them.

Materialism

- Unfortunately, this is a deeply rooted part of modern society.

- People are placed in classes based on their material possessions and our whole life is now destined to run after objects of which we could live without.

- Manipulators use this aspect to their advantage.

- They give materials and objects to their victims to be happy and grateful to this person and begin to follow him in everything they do without objecting a single time.

- Be very careful of all those who seem so nice to you even if they know little about you because they are just trying to buy your trust.

[84]

CHAPTER 12:

What is Dark Psychology?

Psychology underpins everything in our lives, from advertising to finance, crime to religion, and even from hate to love. Someone who can understand these psychological principles is someone who holds onto the key to human influence.

Learning all of the different principles of psychology is not necessary. Start with the lessons in these pages, and you'll have a solid foundation. You have to be able to read people, understand what makes them tick, and understand why they may react in ways that may not be normally expected. And even then, you may need to spend time taking classes and reading through countless books to gain a complete understanding.

So, if only a few people understand psychology and how the human mind works, why is it so important to know what this is? Those who know what it is and how to use it can choose to use that power and that knowledge against you.

While some people are going to use these dark psychology tactics to harm their victim, there are times when you may use these tactics without the intent of negatively manipulating another person. Some of these tactics were intentionally or not added to different variety of means that could include:

- When you were a child, you would see how adults, especially those close to you, behaved.

- When you were a teenager, the mind and your ability to understand the behaviors around you expanded truly.

- You were able to watch others use the tactics and then succeed.

- Using the tactics may have been unintentional in the beginning. Still, when you found that it worked to get you what you wanted, you would start to use those tactics intentionally.

- Some people, such as a politician, a public speaker, or a salesperson, would be trained to handle these types of tactics to get what they want.

Dark Psychology Tactics That Are Used Regularly

- **Love flooding:** This would include any buttering up, praising, or complimenting people to get them to comply with the request that you want. If you want someone to help you move some items into your home, you may use love flooding to make them feel good, making it more likely that they will help you. A dark manipulator could also make the other person feel attached to them and then get them to do things they may not normally do.

- **Lying**: This would include telling the victim an untrue version of the situation. It can also add a partial truth or exaggeration to get what you wanted.

- **Love denial:** This one can be hard on the victim because it can make them feel lost and abandoned by the manipulator. This one includes withholding affection and love until you can get what you want out of the victim.

- **Withdrawal:** This would be when the victim is given the silent treatment or is avoided until they meet the other person's needs.

- **Restricting choices:** The manipulator may give their victims access to some options, but they do this to distract them from the options they don't want the victim to make.

- **Semantic manipulation:** This is a technique where the manipulator is going to use some commonly known words that have accepted meanings by both parties in a conversation. But then they will tell the victim, later on, that they had meant something completely different when they used it.

- **Reverse psychology**: This is when you tell someone to do something in one manner, knowing that they will do the opposite. But the opposite action is what the manipulator wanted to happen in the first place.

Who Will Deliberately Use Dark Tactics?

Many different people may choose to use these dark tactics against you.

They can be found in many various aspects of your life, which is why it is so important to learn how to stay away from them.

Some of the people who can use some of these dark psychology tactics deliberately include:

- **Narcissists:** These individuals are going to have a bloated sense of their self-worth, and they will need to make others believe that they are superior. To meet their desires of being worshipped and adored by everyone they meet, they will use persuasion and dark psychology.

- **Sociopaths:** Those who are sociopaths are charming, intelligent, and persuasive. But they only act this way to get what they want. They lack any emotions, and they are not able to feel any remorse.

  This means that they have no issue using dark psychology tactics to get what they want, including taking it as far as creating superficial relationships.

- **Politicians:** With the help of dark psychology, a politician could convince someone to cast votes for them merely by convincing them that their point of view is the right one.

- **Salespeople:** Not all salespeople are going to use shady tactics against you. But it is possible that some, especially those who are getting their sales numbers and being the best, will not think twice about using dark persuasion to manipulate people.

- **Leaders:** Throughout history, there have been plenty of leaders who will use dark psychology to get their team members, subordinates, and citizens to do what they want.

- **Selfish people:** This could be any person you come across who will make sure that their own needs are put before anyone else's. They aren't concerned about others, and they will let others forego their benefits so that they can benefit.

If the situation helps them, it is okay if it helps someone else. But if someone will be the loser, it will be the other person and not them.

How Is Dark Psychology Used Today?

- When you were a child, you would see how adults, especially those close to you, behaved.

- When you were a teenager, the mind and your ability to understand the behaviors around you were expanded indeed.

- You were able to watch others use the tactics and then succeed.

- Using the tactics may have been unintentional in the beginning, but when you found that it worked to get you what you wanted, you would start to use those tactics intentionally.

- Some people, such as a politician, a public speaker, or a salesperson, would be trained to use these types of tactics to get what they want.

Broad, Practical and Theoretical Observations

Murder, rape, incest, abuse are all words that can send chills up your spine. As a culture, we have saturated ourselves with contrary ideals for entertainment purposes. We sit and watch horror movies, crime shows, and reality shows, diving into the deviant's minds. The darkness within these becomes an obsession for some, and though they don't reenact or find the actions preferable, there is a connection that few want to recognize outwardly. While most human beings have a buffer in their mind, knowing fact from fiction and right from wrong, some lack it.

Imagination is one thing. Combining people's worst fears to find what scenario can be the scariest and most grabbing is something fiction writers and creators do. Often, though, when watching these dark psyches at work on the screen in front of you, the human mind finds a specific recognition of why the predator or villain did what they did. Some movies and books even prey on the idea of the worst human condition. Depraved and distraught, the father who witnessed his family's murders climbs out of his ominous depression to wreak havoc on those that committed the acts to begin with. There is satisfaction for people in the revenge of heinous acts. But then, doesn't that apply the same dark psyche to the perpetrator, regardless of the reasoning behind it?

Dark Psychology has no pointed targets and cares little for the reasoning behind the actions. It is the actual act of manipulation, deceit, and harm that carries the dark psyche's weight. The idea of revenge has been around for a very long time. Some significant points in history are considered a requirement of honor if the wrong was done to you. Prominent examples of the "eye for an eye" concept are still in existence today. The death penalty is one such example, though its root is broad and doesn't currently encourage one person's private actions to another. The federal organization as a whole is in charge of carrying out the punishment. But long before that, laws were erected in civilizations that based themselves on the idea of revenge.

Psychological Definition

The human condition is studied continuously, broken down, dissected, and used in the psychological community. Dark Psychology subscribes to this as well. However, in dark psychology studies, its focus relates to the nature of the predator vs. prey relationship of the human condition. Psychologists focusing on the dark psyche move their research toward people who perpetrate crimes or abnormal activity with little or no instinct or care of the social norms. Most people have that buffer protecting others from these ideals, while the perpetrators lack this ability to keep control of their most basic sexual instincts.

You may be thinking that basic instincts do not include the often heinous acts performed by someone with a dark psyche. And while you are correct, there is a significant difference with the .01% of criminal acts performed by dark minds of particular interest, and if you think about the most primal human from millions of years ago, they lacked one major player that we all deem reasonable. The very early primitive human beings did not have a societal construct that had been bored into them from birth, augmented with religious ideals, and regulated by high functioning governments. Their most primal instinct was survival.

In a world fraught with danger, both natural and nurturing, the human mind protected the body at all costs. There were most likely times that manipulating and deceit are worse committed in an uncalled for the situation. However, our brains are wired to perceive danger and either act on that or flee. Survival back then had more to do with the ability to fight off animals and find food, water, and shelter. There were no other societal norms.

Since our brains are the same brains inside the Neanderthal man, our perception of danger is the only thing that has changed. In a world where almost everyone has food, water, and shelter at their disposal, the fight for those types of situations is lower. In today's society, we see the instinct of survival manipulated into a course where we fight for more, better, and more. Frequently the crimes committed outside of the realm of revenge or the .01 percent are based solely on those theories.

CHAPTER 13:

How People Use Dark Psychology

Let us look at some of the people who use dark psychology tactics the most.

1. Salespeople: These are some of the main users who we meet daily. They use advertisements, door to door campaigns, Professional language, and any other tool they can access to persuade us to purchase a particular thing. This mostly applies to the salespeople who are so obsessed with reaching a target that they do anything to make people buy their products

2. **Sociopaths (Those who meet the clinical diagnosis):** People who are truly psychopathic lack the ability to feel remorse and a sense of emotionality. On the other side, these people are often intelligent, charming, and yet impulsive. They use these characteristics to their advantage by using Dark psychology tactics to build extra strong relationships with people they later take advantage of without second thought.

3. **Attorneys:** Most of the attorneys are focused on winning a case. As such, they use many tactics to get the results they desire. Some attorneys resort to dark persuasion techniques.

4. **Narcissists:** The people who meet the term narcissist's clinical definition have an inflated sense of self-worth. Normally, they need other people to praise them and rub their ego. The narcissist wants everyone to believe that he/she is superior to them. He/she desires to adored and worshipped excessively. As a result, the narcissist will use

any tactic, including dark psychology persuasion and unethical manipulation, to have followers.

5. **Politicians**: A large number of politicians are selfish and will do anything to get votes. They sometimes turn to dark psychology techniques to convince people about what they believe.

6. **Leaders**: Some leaders and managers use dark tactics to get others to comply and act in a particular way.

7. **Selfish people**: Some people only have a self-centered plan and will do anything to get what they want. In some cases, these people may use Tactics to meet their needs without caring about others' consequences.

8. **Public speakers**: You might be wondering how a public speaker whose intention is to help the people become better can use dark tactics. Well, they can. Sometimes, some speakers use dark tactics to get more followers and even sell more products.

Yes, I know I might have stepped on some toes by mentioning the above people, but it is important to know the basics. Attorneys, public speakers, salespersons, leaders, and all the other people are trying to make a living. However, they need to be honest about their work and avoid using manipulative tactics. As a potential victim, you need to identify when a person uses manipulative and dark psychology techniques for good or bad intentions.

A salesperson can make more sales for a company by using dark psychology and manipulative tactics. Some salespeople admit that their organizations train and require them to use dark psychology to meet targets, get customers, and retain them. This is unfortunate. Although the company will get revenue, it will finally lead to poor business practices, distrust, poor employee loyalty, and less long-term success.

To differentiate between ethical and unethical motivation and persuasion techniques, one must assess his/her intentions. You need to ask yourself, are these techniques benefiting all of us, or is it just one person? It is okay for the techniques to help you alongside other people, but it is unethical to use these techniques selfishly. It is easy to fall into using dark techniques if intentions are entirely selfish.

The first step to avoiding using dark psychology for selfish intention is to aim for a win-win situation. A salesperson should aim to sell a product that will benefit the customer. He/she should be able to stay honest with the customer. In most cases, the salesperson seeks to tell the potential customer about the benefits of these products so that he/she can make a purchase.

If you are a leader, a salesperson, a marketer, or any one of these people who might fall into using dark psychology techniques for self-centered purposes, you need to ask yourself.

- What is my intention or goal in this interaction?

- Do my actions benefit anyone else, or is it just me?

- Do I feel good about my approach to this interaction?

- Am I open and honest with the other person?

- Will, the results of this conversation be beneficial to everyone in the long-term?

- In the end, will I have a healthier and more trusting relationship with this person?

Such self-analysis will help a person to avoid using selfish, dark psychology techniques on others. If you truly want to be successful in relationships, career, leadership work, parenting, and other areas of life, you need to assess your current tactics for persuasion and motivation. Doing the right thing in the right way will lead to long term positive influence and credibility. Using dark techniques to get what you want might help you for a while, but in the long term, you will lose, have broken relationships, have poor character, and lose credibility because people will see through the mask. Keep in mind the fact that more people are learning dark psychology and how to identify its users. More people are learning how to be emotionally intelligent to avoid manipulation and unethical manipulation.

As mentioned earlier, dark psychology is the art of manipulation and persuasion. According to criminologists, dark psychology is a branch of study covering the human conditions that relate to people's nature preying on others motivated by deviant or criminal drives that lack a win-win drive. Technically, all of humanity has the potential to make other victims of selfish motives. The only difference is that some people suppress their dark side while others act on the impulses.

As a study, dark psychology seeks to understand these thoughts, perceptions, feelings, and subjective processes that lead people to predatory behavior. What makes one behave in an antithetical manner that defies contemporary human behavior? Dark psychology explains that deviant, criminal, and abusive behavior is purposive and has some rational and goal-oriented motive ninety-nine percent of the time. The remaining 1 % is assumed to be the region in the human psyche that enables some of us to commit atrocious acts with or without purpose.

CHAPTER 14:

The Basics on How to Read Anyone

The first part of being able to influence and manipulate someone will be when you learn how to read them. You have to get a good analysis on the other person, or you are going to end up with a lot of trouble in the process trying to get them to do what you want or wasting time with a strategy that doesn't work for that particular target.

The good news is that there are quite a few steps that you can take to figure out who someone is so that you can learn more about them and pick out the right manipulation technique to get what you want. So, let's dive right into the best steps that anyone can use when learning how to read anyone!

Learning the Baseline of the Target

The first thing that we need to be able to do here is to learn how to get a baseline on the target we wish to work with. The baseline is just going to be when we notice how the person usually behaves when they are not stressed out, overly happy, or have any other reason to act in a different way than what is normal.

While it is common to learn how to watch out for body language to help us know whether the other person likes us or lying or not, you will find that not everyone will behave in the same manner under those circumstances. When you can take some time to learn the baseline of the target, you will learn how they are going to behave regularly, and then it is easier to catch when there are changes to that behavior.

For example, you may notice that someone is acting a bit jumpy around you and wonder what is going on. For most people, this is a sign that they are anxious or waiting for something to happen. But, when you spend some time learning the other person's baseline, you may notice that they are always jumpy. If that person is usually jumpy, then this kind of jumpiness will not tell you much. But if that person is a jumpy kind of being, and you notice that they suddenly stay still instead of moving around, then this is a sign that there is something up with them.

Each person will be a little bit different from one another, which is why it is so important to start and try to find their baseline, rather than assuming that you already know everything about the other person and that they know nothing at all. If you jump to conclusions and don't pay attention to what you can get out of the other person, you will find that it is hard to know when things are normal and off.

Figuring out the baseline of your target is going to be so important to helping you read their body language. But, it is something that a lot of people are going to miss out on. They need to take some time to practice it long before they even waste their time trying to figure out what one action means over another.

A good way to get some practice is to look for this baseline, even before you go out and pick a target to manipulate. The next time you interact in some manner with another person and have a conversation with them, take a moment to notice things like where their hands are, how they are positioning their feet, and even the amount they smile. Don't take note or anything because this is going to seem odd, but just get in the habit of being more observant of what is going on around you. Of course, the more times you can practice this, the easier it is. And once you have that nice baseline down, you will find that it is much easier for you to find a target, pinpoint the baseline that they have, and then you can easily notice the changes to their body language when these come up.

Learn the Different Personality Types

We need to take a look at some of the different personality types that we need to have to help us get to know the target. The truth is, every person you encounter is going to be a little bit different from the others, and this is fine. Learning who they are and why they react to things in a certain way is going to be hard to get each time because all of us are created to be unique and special.

With that said, several personality types are recognized at large, and we all are going to lean closer to one of them, or one combination of them than the other. You can use these different types of personalities, and the things that come with them, to help you get a little bit better feel of the target you are trying to analyze.

Here, we are going to take a look at the four groups of personalities, which include four sub-sects of personalities within them. You may find that someone fits a little bit of more than one of these, and that is just fine. Learning the basics of them and trying to understand how each one works is not always exact, but it can give you a better idea of the person you are dealing with ahead of time.

First, we have the analysts. These will be the people who like to study things and are going to rely a lot on the facts presented to them. They have emotions, but they are not going to base any decisions they make on these emotions. This means that you should not waste your time with emotional tactics to get them to do what you want. Instead, if you can get them many facts about why they should react one way over another, you are more likely to get the results you want.

There are four types of personalities that tend to fit under the umbrella of the analyst. Some of the personality types that fit in with the analyst will include:

Architect: This kind of person is going to be a thinker who is strategic and imaginative. They like to think things through, and they are going to come up with a plan for everything.

Logician: This will be the kind of person who is an inventor and has an unquenchable thirst for as much knowledge as possible.

Commander: These people like to be the one that is in charge. They are bold and imaginative, and they are going to be strong-willed leaders. They will either find a way or they are going to make their way to get it done.

Next on the list is going to be the diplomat. These are the people who can think things through in a way that is going to benefit other people, and not just themselves. They use logic, but there is often a bit of emotion in the mix. If you want to manipulate this kind of person, you have to be ready to add in some facts coupled with emotion and more. çThey are an interesting group to work with, and you will find that reading them will give you a lot of the good practice you are looking for. Some of the personality types that are going to fit in with the diplomat are going to include:

The advocate: This person is going to be pretty quiet and mystical. And yet, you will find that they are also very inspiring and tireless idealists.

Mediator: This kind of person is going to be poetic, altruistic, and kind in most situations that come around them. They love it when they can help out with what they see as a good cause.

Protagonist: This kind of person is going to be charismatic and can inspire others when they are the leader. And they can mesmerize the people who are listening to them.

Campaigner: This is going to be a free spirit who is friendly, creative, and enthusiastic. They are really good to be around because they know how to make you smile about anything.

When you find that the person you are reading does not fit into any of the categories above, then maybe they are considered a sentinel. These will be like the guards; the ones who are going to help defend others will help rule and provide counsel when needed. You will find that these kinds of people will be reliable all of the time, making them good çfriends but can sometimes make them more susceptible to the manipulation techniques you use. Some of the examples that are out there for a sentinel personality group include:

Logistician: This kind of person will focus on the facts and think critically about everything. When it comes to their reliability, you can always trust what they are telling you and that they will do what they promise.

The defender: This kind of person is going to be a kind of protector. They are really warm and dedicated to whatever they put their minds to. They will always be there to defend the ones they love the most or those they think they are closest to.

Executive: These people are going to be great at managing things and people, and they are some of the best administrators around, even if you don't want them to manage all of these things.

Consul: The final personality type that fits under this umbrella term will be the consul. This kind of person is going to be very popular, social, and caring. They are always there to help out others, almost to a fault, and you know that they have your back when it is needed.

CHAPTER 15:

What Is NLP (Neuro-Linguistic Programming)? A Method to Enhance Personal Development

The acronym NLP stands for neuro-linguistic programming and indicates a methodology for changing one or more people's thoughts and behaviors to help them achieve the desired results. Born in the 70s in California in the middle of the New Age era, NLP owes its success to the promise (often kept) to improve work performance and achieve happiness through personal development. The founders of NLP, the psychologist Richard Bundler and the linguist John Grinder, started from the belief that they could identify successful individuals' thought patterns and behaviors and then teach them to others.

One of NLP's main techniques is constituted by imitation or, as adepts define it, modeling: by imitating the language and behaviors of successful people, it would be possible to make our skills our own and achieve their results.

NLP is mainly based on language processing and uses other communication techniques to make people change their thoughts and behaviors.

How Does it Work?

- NLP is based on the idea that people operate through internal "maps" to represent the world.

- NLP thus tries to identify these maps (which are nothing more than subjective experiences of what surrounds us) to change their orientations. It is a methodology that aims at a change of thought and behavior.

- It should be specified that NLP has nothing to do with hypnosis. On the contrary, it works through the conscious use of language to modify a person's mental and behavioral patterns.

What Is It For?

- NLP finds a wide field of intervention, using various techniques according to the desired purposes.

- Starting from the idea that thought and behavior can be modeled, NLP is used for:

- Treat anxiety, phobias, and stress, thus improving emotional responses to certain situations;

- Achieve successful professional goals, such as increased productivity at work and motivation;

- Remove negative thoughts and feelings associated with a past event;

- Improve their communication skills.

- In general, NLP is used as a personal development method through the "enhancement" of one's skills, which aims to have greater self-confidence and communicate better with others.

The Criticisms

To date, the efficacy of NLP has not yet been demonstrated, although more than 40 years have passed since its conception, nor has this practice been the subject of rigorous scientific analysis, as happened, for example, for cognitive psychological therapy- behavioral. This has led to an absence of formal regulation, giving rise to both arbitrary interpretations of the method and its "manipulative" use.

Furthermore, scientific research on NLP has found contradictory evidence.

Some studies from the 1980s to 1990s have proven the benefits associated with NLP. For example, a study published in the journal Counselling and Psychotherapy Research found that patients in psychotherapy (various addresses) had improved symptoms and quality of life after being treated in association with the NLP methodology and psychotherapeutic treatments.

However, a review published in the 2014 British Journal of General Practice refutes NLP's effectiveness with at least 10 studies. In summary, according to these studies, there is little evidence to assert that the method works with demonstrative evidence, especially when it intends to treat people's health, including mood disorders, weight management, and substance abuse. According to scholars, the positive effects on the method's impact would exist, but they are not exhaustive and not convincing. Only 18% of all research on NLP found clear cause-and-effect support for the theories underlying the method.

- However, it should be noted that the research was conducted mainly in therapeutic contexts and not in the commercial context, where NLP would find greater use.

- One of the most used communication techniques in the last twenty years is Neuro-Linguistic Programming. Known as NLP, it is one of the "sciences" most used by researchers, athletes, consultants, managers, training experts, and professional communicators.

- NLP was born and developed in California in the 70s, thanks to the collaboration of the mathematician Richard Bundler and the famous linguist Jhon Grinder.

- Reserved for a few in the past because of the high cost of the courses and the books' difficulty that dealt with the subject, this science gradually manages to make its way into the psychological sphere.

What is NLP Exactly?

It is a psychological method that studies people's behavior, analyses models, and thus extracts the practical techniques to teach to potentially overcome any situation (work, success, relationships).

NLP teaches that each of us can, with willpower, change and revolutionize one's life in an instant, abandoning limits through the help of concrete techniques. Each person is the architect of his destiny, determined exclusively by our decisions and not by the living conditions as many believe and which are already "prescribed" and not changeable.

NLP's message to us is the secret of living well, which is "living life trying to make the most of it." It is we, and only us, who can make everything we want possible, starting from the determination and constancy, which from the beginning must not be missing, together with the desire to fight for a purpose, therefore the energy that goes put into practice, up to the exercise, application, construction, and achievement of our goal.

In a nutshell, this method would help us become the people we always wanted to be; an opportunity to learn how to use our mind and body in the most functional way possible.

Talking about NLP is equivalent to dealing with themes based on creativity, freedom, self-esteem, choices, and courage. The founders of NLP coined this term (Neuro-Linguistic Programming) precisely to highlight a link between neurological processes (neuro), language (linguistics), and the various behavioral screens that have been learned only through experience (programming). It is indeed impossible, according to Bundler and Grinder, to find a field where this model cannot be applied: From self-esteem problems to sports or school skills, from courtship to success, and some even claim that this discipline somehow manages to fight depression and other psychological disorders. Summing up, NLP has among its main purposes, the goal of developing successful habits/reactions, amplifying effective behaviors to make what we want for us to happen, and decreasing unwanted ones, which limit the occurrence of our design drawings. With Neuro-Linguistic Programming, you learn to model the quality of the internal images lived and the sensations perceived so that they act for our benefit in the future. NLP makes us aware of our unconscious behaviors and programs that we can modify as we wish.

There are NLP academies where you can learn and put into practice all the possible techniques to achieve what you want a purpose: motivation, the basis for all our desire, is the ingredient that pushes us to fight to get it. Without it, none of us would be able to reach the end to which it aspires.

- Do you want to understand who you are facing in 60 seconds?

- Do you want to sell successfully?

- Would you like to increase your charisma or have a seductive and convincing voice?

- According to the method in question, this can be done and much more.

Optimism, the joy of life, and cooperation are the three secrets of living in harmony. Everyone needs a paladin.

Have you ever wished for some things for yourself and done nothing to get what you claim you want? Have you ever wanted to lose weight, to free yourself from the slavery of some addiction such as alcohol or smoking, to want to learn a language or play an instrument?

Certainly yes, but how many of you have put your goals into practice, and how many others have been stuck? This is how it happens, for all those belonging to the second sphere, who finds us doing only one action: complaining. The coach then takes over and helps us take stock, find our orientation, define ourselves as people. It spurs us to find motivation if our "journey" becomes tortuous.

There are four types of coaches:

Life Coach: the one who helps us achieve personal goals

Company Coach: the one who helps companies and professionals in the sector to act more effectively and with determination in professional life

Career Coach: one who helps people in the phases of professional change, therefore a career jump or even a professional regression

Sports Coach: helps students raise the level of performance and thus triggers mental and physical training

Therefore, the main objective of NLP is to explain to us how everything we are is the simple result of what we have thought. Our life is in our hands.

- Don't believe it? Try it for yourself!

- NLP is an attitude

Characterized by a sense of curiosity, adventure, and desire to learn the necessary skills to understand what communication types affect others. It is the desire to know things that are worth knowing. It is looking at life as a rare opportunity to learn.

NLP Is a Methodology

Based on the principle that every behavior has a structure and that this structure can be extrapolated, learned, taught, and even changed. The guiding criterion of this method is to know what will be useful and effective.

NLP Is a Technology

- This allows a person to organize information and perceptions to achieve results deemed impossible in the past.

- Neuro-Linguistic Programming, therefore, deals with studying the structure of subjective experience and what can be calculated from it.

- His basic belief and promise are that effective thinking strategies can be identified, assumed, and used by anyone who wishes to.

- NLP was born from the fruit of years of research, carried out by Richard Bundler and John Grinder, to find out what the behavioral and linguistic elements were that allowed successful people to have such a significant constancy of positive results.

- The results were the identification of a series of specific and reproducible behavioral strategies and linguistic models.

The Hoaxes of Neuro-Linguistic Programming

From psychotherapy to coaching, NLP is still without solid experimental evidence and has many characteristics of pseudosciences.

Neuro-linguistic programming (NLP) has been rejected by science in every possible and imaginable way, yet it continues to be talked about.

The more attentive will have noticed that in the film Kingsman: Secret service (2014), neuro-linguistic programming is passed off as a seduction weapon.

It is almost impossible to find a field where the NLP, according to its supporters, cannot be applied: from courtship to leadership, from self-esteem problems to sports skills, success is at hand, and there are even those who come to propose discipline to combat depression and other psychological disorders.

But what exactly is neuro-linguistic programming?

The Origins

The NLP was born in the first half of the 70s, the golden age of the New-Age, and perhaps it is no coincidence that the crib was the California lysergic. The dads in the new discipline were Richard Bundler, a psychology student at the time, and linguist John Grinder, both from the University of California, Santa Cruz, who had begun to work out a sort of 'theory of everything' of psychotherapy from their respective fields. Of study.

One of the cornerstones of the new, revolutionary branch of psychology would be imitation or, as the adepts define it, modeling: imitating successful people's language and behavior it would be possible to make our skills our own and achieve their results.

CHAPTER 16:

Brainwashing

This zone will center in travel toward brainwashing and the entirety of the parts that go with it. Through the media and the movies that are seen, different people consider brainwashing to be a mischievous practice done by the people trying to weaken, influence, and gain power. Some who truly have faith in brainwashing power recognize that people, including them, are endeavoring to control their minds and their lead. Generally, the course toward brainwashing happens in a by and large progressively unobtrusive way. It excludes the horrendous practices that many people unite with it. This part will significantly affect what brainwashing is and how it can influence the subject's perspective.

What Is Brainwashing?

Brainwashing right currently is talked about like its use in psychology. At this moment, it is recommended as a strategy for out and out considered change social impact. This sort of social effect is happening for the range of the day to each person, paying little notification to whether they get it or not. Social impact is the accumulation of procedures used to change others' practices, emotions, and tempers. For example, consistent frameworks used in the working environment could be viewed as brainwashing since they envision that you should act and think a specific way when you are occupied with working. Brainwashing can wind up being a progressively conspicuous degree, a social issue in its most certifiable structure considering how these systems work at changing how someone thinks without the subject consenting to it.

For brainwashing to work successfully, the subject will need to experience hard and fast separation and reliance because of its noticeable contact concerning the issue. This is one explanation that huge amounts of the brainwashing cases that are considered happen in totalistic religions or prison camps. The brainwasher, or the executive, must have the decision to increase endless oversight over their subject. This surmises they should control the dietary examples, snoozing structures, and satisfy the subject's other human needs. None of these activities can happen without the desire for power. During this technique, the chairman will work to profitably confine the subject's entire character to make it not work right any more fundamentally. When the character is broken, the ace will abolish it with the ideal sentiments, tempers, and practices.

The course toward brainwashing is still helpfully discredited, whether it will work. Most clinicians hold the emotions that it is conceivable to intellectually program a subject as long as the correct conditions are open. Also, at last, the entire technique isn't as absurd as it has appeared in the media. There are different implications of brainwashing that make it logically difficult to pick the impacts of brainwashing concerning the issue. A piece of these definitions requires that there must be a sort of hazard to the physical body of the subject to be viewed as brainwashing. On the off chance that you look for after this definition, even the practices done by different fan religions would not be viewed as clear brainwashing as no physical abuse happens. Different implications of brainwashing will depend upon control and threatening without physical power to modify the subjects' sentiments. Notwithstanding, specialists recognize that the impact of brainwashing, significantly under the perfect conditions, is only a passing occasion. They recognize that the subject's old character isn't obliterated with the preparation; rather, it is set into concealing and will return once the new character isn't fortified anymore.

Robert Jay Lifton arranged some fascinating contemplations on brainwashing for the 1950s after reviewing prisoners of the Chinese and Korean War camps. During his observations, he concluded that these prisoners experienced a multistep system of brainwashing. This approach started with assaults on the notion of self with the prisoner and, starting their onward, finished with an alleged change in the subject's sentiments. There are ten stages that Lifton depicted by the brainwashing system in the subjects that he investigated. These included:

1. A snare on the character of the subject

2. Forcing issue concerning the issue

3. Forcing the subject into self-shamefulness

4. Reaching a limit

5. Offering the subject opposition if they change

6. Compulsion to concede

7. Channeling the accuse the ordinary way

8. Releasing the subject of acknowledged issue

9. Progressing to comprehension

10. The last confirmation before a restoration

These stages must occur in a zone that is in finished isolation. This construes the vast majority of the conventional social references that the subject is familiar with interfacing, which is difficult to reach. Besides, mind darkening structures will be used to quicken the procedure, for example, nonappearance of strong sustenance and nonattendance of rest. While this may not be considered for all brainwashing cases, typically, there is a closeness of physical mischief, which adds to the objective of experiencing speculation issues uninhibitedly and fundamentally like they normally would.

Steps Used

While Lifton isolated the brainwashing system's strategies into ten stages, present-day consultants mastermind it into three phases to even more plausible handle what continues for the subject during this procedure. These three phases consolidate the separating of oneself, acquainting the opportunity of salvation with the subject, and then re-trying the subject's self. Seeing these stages and the system that occurs with every one of them can help you understand what is coming upon the character of the subject with this methodology.

Separating of the Self

The central theme of the brainwashing strategy is fundamentally the separating of the self. During this procedure, the manager needs to disconnect the subject's old character to cause them to feel dynamically slight and open to the ideal new character. This development is fundamental to continue on the technique. The chairman won't be staggeringly profitable with their undertakings if the subject is still unequivocally set in their motivation and old character. Separating this character and making the individual solicitation the things around them can make it less intricate to change the character in the later advances. This is done through two or three phases recollecting attack for the subject's character, bringing on an issue, self-misleading, and sometimes later appears at the limit.

Ambush on Identity

The ambush on the subject's character is fundamentally the specific assault regarding the issues' inclination of self or their interior identity or character alongside their center game-plan of conviction. It makes the subject solicitation what their character is by causing them to envision that all that they have ever acknowledged isn't right. The professional will contribute a lot of essentialness, denying everything that the subject is. In prisoner camps, for example, the manager will offer expressions like "You are certainly not making sure about circumstance," "You are not a man," and "You are not a warrior." The subject will be under ambushes like these consistently for a genuinely long time up to months. This is done all things considered as to deplete the subjects with the target that they become amazed, bewildered, and depleted. Precisely when the subject appears at this sort of expression, their emotions will begin to have all the reserves of being less strong, and they may begin to recognize the things that they are told.

Fault

When the subject has experienced the ambush on their character, they will enter the deficiency time. The subject will be constantly instructed that they are dreadful while experiencing this new character emergency encouraged. This does all things considered to encourage an enormous estimation of the issue to the subject. The subject will be continually persisting through an assault for any of the things they have done, offering little appreciation of how colossal or little the showings might be.

The degree of the assaults can change; moreover, the subject could be criticized for their conviction structures to how they dress and even consider how they eat too bit by bit. After some time, the subject will begin to feel disregard around them continually, and they will feel that everything they are doing isn't right. This can cause them to feel powerfully slight and slanted to oblige the new character the master needs to make.

Self-selling out

Since the subject has been convinced that they are dreadful and that a large portion of their activities is infuriating, the master is quitting any funny business to propel the subject to yield that they are awful. Directly, the subject is stifling in their shortcoming and feeling confounded. Through the length of the psychological ambushes, the danger of some inconceivable physical insidiousness, or a mix of the two, the star will have the decision to drive the subject to blame his old character. This can join a wide combination of things, such as getting the subject to accuse their mates, sidekicks, and family who offer a near conviction framework. While this framework may require a tremendous period to happen, when it does, the subject will feel like he duped those that he feels devoted to. This will develop the lack of regard comparably as the loss of character that the objective is beginning at now feeling, further separating the subject's character.

Breaking point

By this point, the subject is feeling confined and confounded. They may introduce demands, for example, Where am I? Who am I? Besides, what may it be judicious for me to do? The subject is in a character emergency now and is experiencing some significant insolence. Since they have misled many of the emotions and the people he has continually known, the subject will experience a psychological crisis.

In psychology, this reasonable technique a social occasion of certifiable appearances that consistently show a massive number of expected mental disturbing effects. A touch of the signs can fuse general confusion, significant wretchedness, and uncontrolled groaning. The subject may have the notions of being lost alongside having a free handle on this current reality. When the subject appears at this breaking point, they will have lost their opinion of themselves. The manager will fundamentally choose to do anything they need with them now since the subject has lost their comprehension of what's happening around them and their personality. In a like way now, the ace will set up the different allurements that are significant to change over the subject towards another conviction structure. The new framework will be set up to offer salvation to the subject from the wretchedness that they are feeling.

CHAPTER 17:

Hypnosis

While brainwashing is a bewildering kind of mind control that different people have pondered, hypnosis is likewise a fundamental sort that should be considered. For the most part, the people who consider hypnosis consider it from watching stage shows of people doing senseless acts. While this is a kind of hypnosis, there is fundamentally more to it. This region is going to concentrate more on hypnosis as a kind of mind control.

What Is Hypnosis?

Regardless, is the massiveness of hypnosis? According to masters, hypnosis is seen as a condition of mindfulness that joins the pulled in thought near the diminished periphery care portrayed by the part's comprehensive capacity to respond to the proposition given. This prescribes the part that will enter a substitute point of view and will be astonishingly continuously vulnerable against look for after the recommendations that are given by the surprise inducer.

It is conventionally seen that two hypotheses pack help outline what's happening during the hypnosis timespan. The first is known as the reasonable state speculation. After this theory, the people who search for hypnosis see that hypnosis takes after a stupor or a viewpoint that is changed where the part will see that their consideration is adequately not equivalent to what they would discover in their standard mindful state. The unmistakable theory is the non-state speculations. After this theory, the people who search for this theory don't recognize that the people who experience hypnosis are going into different conditions of perception. Perhaps, the part is working with the stunning capacity to enter a kind of imaginative development foundation. While in hypnosis, the part is thought to have more fixation and focus than couples and another ability to concentrate on a specific memory or thought unequivocally. During this technique, the part is in like route orchestrated to polish off different sources that may incorporate them. The entranced subjects are thought to demonstrate a raised ability to respond to the recommendation given to them, especially when these propositions start from the trance inducer. The system used to place the part into hypnosis is known as rest inciting selection and will join an improvement of recommendations and headings used as a kind of warm-up. The authorities raise different contemplations concerning what the vitality of hypnosis is. The wide collection of these definitions starts because there are such endless different conditions that go with hypnosis. Nobody has an identical experience when encountering it. A section of the different ramifications of hypnosis by pros solidify the going with:

1. "A stand-apart occasion of mental fall away from the confidence," Michael Nash.

2. Ernest Hilgard and Janet Hilgard have written in unprecedented Significance about hypnosis and depict it as a course for the body to isolate itself in another plane of mindfulness.

3. Sarbin and Coe, two comprehended social clinicians, have to use business theory to depict hypnosis. Under this definition, the part is envisioning being enchanted; they act like they are mesmerized instead of truly being in that state.

4. According to T.X. Beautician, hypnosis is delineated at risk to the unmistakable nonhypnotic social parameters. Under this definition, the part will depict the endeavor inspiration and etching the condition that they are hypnosis since they have no other thing to call it.

5. Weitzenhoffer wrote in a few of his past works about hypnosis. He conceptualized that hypnosis is a condition of improved suggestibility. In later pieces, he continued portraying the demonstration of hypnosis as "a sort of effect by one individual applied on another through the medium or office of the proposition.

6. Brenman and Gill used the psychoanalytic thought of "break confidence in the association of the psychological self-view" to help delineate what hypnosis was about. Under this definition, the part is fretful to go under hypnosis and into the fair state since it helps their psychological self-picture and improves them to feel.

7. According to Edmonston, a person who has experienced hypnosis is basically in a puzzle to remove up.

8. Spiegel and Spiegel have conveyed that hypnosis is fundamentally something that occurs in context on the commonplace most remote scopes of the part.

9. Erickson states that hypnosis is a balanced, internally supported, and wonderful condition of working. The part is starting quite recently masterminded to work and ponders things around them. Regardless, they are in a not too bad state that stood separated from their normal state.

There are different points of view and pronouncements that have been made about hypnosis. A couple of people perceive that hypnosis is genuine and are suspicious that the association and others around them will attempt to control their minds. Others don't have confidence in hypnosis at all and envision that it is fit deluding. Likely, the authenticity of hypnosis as mind control falls in some spot in the middle. There are multiple times of hypnosis that are seen by the psychological framework. These three stages fuse affirmation, suggestion, and weakness.

Enrollment

The fundamental time of hypnosis is an affirmation. Before the part encounters the full hypnosis, they will be familiar with the rest actuating affirmation framework. For a long time, this was recognized as the strategy used to put the subject into their trancelike trance; at any rate, that definition has changed some. A dash of the non-state examiners has seen this stage, maybe in an astounding manner. Or on the other hand, possibly they acknowledge this to be as the framework to broaden the people's requirements for what will happen, delineating the development that they will play, standing isolated enough to be accepted to focus the right way and any of different advances that are required to lead the part into the right bearing for hypnosis.

There are a few determination systems that can be used during hypnosis. The most extraordinary and convincing frameworks are Braid's "eye obsession" technique or "Braidism." There are different assortments along these thinking lines, including the Stanford Hypnotic Susceptibility Scale (SHSS). This scale is the most used instrument to look at the field of hypnosis.

To use the Braid determination systems, you should search for after a few phases. The first is to take any object that you can find dazzling, for example, a watch case, and hold it between the inside, fore, and thumb fingers on the left hand. You should hold this thing around 8-15 killjoys from the eyes of the part. Hold the article some spot over the asylums to put a lot of strain on the eyelids and eyes during the framework to keep up a fixed look on the thing constantly.

The unexpected virtuoso should then uncover that they should concentrate their eyes consistently on the thing. The patient will, in like manner, need to concentrate their mind absolutely on that specific article. They should not consider different things or let their cerebrums and eyes wander or probably the framework won't be pivotal.

In a little while, the part's eyes will begin to create. With really additional time, the part will begin to perceive a wavy improvement. On the off possibility that the part typically closes their eyelids when the inside and forefingers of the right hand are given from the eyes to the thing, by then, they are in the daze. If not, by then, the part should begin once more; endeavor to admonish the part that they are to connect with their eyes to close once the fingers are passed on in every practical sense undefined progression back towards the eyes once more. This will get the patient to go into the changed point of view that is known as hypnosis.

While Braid stayed by his structure, he saw that hypnosis's affirmation method isn't constantly basic for each case. Believe it or not, experts presently have usually discovered that the decision framework isn't as basic with the effects of rest beginning suggestions beginning late suspected. After some time, indisputable different decisions and assortments of the boss trancelike affirmation framework have been made, despite the way that the Braid system is starting at as of late considered the best.

Proposition

The going with the time of hypnosis is known as the suggestion mastermind. Unequivocally when James Braid first depicted hypnosis, the term of suggestion was not used. Or, on the other hand, maybe, Braid prescribed this stage as the demonstration of having the clever character of the part base on one central and uncommon idea. The way that Braid did this was to empower or decrease the different locales' physiological working on the part's body. Later on, Braid began to put legitimately more accentuation on using different nonverbal and verbal sorts of recommendations to get the part into the trancelike perspective. These would consolidate using "waking recommendations" equivalently as self-hypnosis.

Another astounding subliminal virtuoso, Hippolyte Bernheim, continued moving the enhancement of the state of being of the procedure for hypnosis over to the psychological framework that contained verbal suggestions. As Bernheim demonstrated, rest affirmation is the determination of a psychical condition that is exceptional and will assemble the deficiency of the suggestion to the part. Regularly, he conferred that the spellbinding state that is induced will engage the suggestion, despite how this plausible won't be fundamental to start the shortcoming regardless.

The current subliminal treatment uses a gathering of recommendation outlines to be useful, for example, depictions, recommendations, slippery or non-verbal proposition, direct verbal suggestions, and obvious fascinating explanations and propositions that are non-verbal. A bit of the non-verbal recommendation used during the proposition stage would join physical control, voice tonality, and mental imagery.

One of the partitions made in the sorts of recommendations that can be offered to the part fuses those suggestions passed on with underwriting and those that despot in the manner.

Something that must be considered for hypnosis is the separation between the missing and the mindful character. There are a few stupor pros who consider them to be of the recommendation as a framework for giving that is guided generally speaking to the subject's keen character. Others in the field will see it the other way; they see the relationship between the professional and the normal or missing character.

CHAPTER 18:

Why Dark Psychology Affects You?

All of us have the possibility for killer habits as well as this potential has accessibility to our thoughts, feelings as well as understandings. As you will undoubtedly read throughout this book, we all have this potential, but just a couple of us act upon them. Everyone has had thoughts as well as sensations, at one time or another, of wishing to work ruthlessly. Most of us have had ideas of wanting to injure others severely without mercy. If you are truthful with your own, you will certainly have to agree you have had thoughts and a sensation of intending to dedicate abhorrent acts.

Provided the truth, we consider ourselves a good-hearted species; one would love to think we believe these ideas, as well as feelings, would be non-existent. Unfortunately, most of us have these thoughts as well, as luckily, we never act on them. Dark Psychology positions some individuals with these very same ideas, feelings, and assumptions but act on them in either conscious or spontaneous means. The noticeable distinction is that they act on them while others just have fleeting thoughts and feelings.

Every one of humanity has the potential to victimize humans and even other living creatures. While numerous limits or sublimate this propensity, some act upon these impulses.

It is the study of the human problem as it connects to people's emotional nature to prey upon others. Dark Psychology looks to understand those ideas, sensations, and understandings that lead to human predacious actions. Dark Psychology thinks that this production is purposive and has some logical, goal-oriented inspiration

99.99% of the time. Under Dark Psychology, the remaining 0, 01% is the harsh victimization of others without a purposive intent or reasonably specified by evolutionary science or religious dogma. Within the following century, predators and their acts of theft, violence, and misuse will come to be a global sensation and societal epidemic otherwise compressed. Religion, philosophy, psychology, and various other convictions have tried cogently to define Dark Psychology. It is true that most human behaviors, related to evil activities, is purposive and objective-oriented. There is a location where purposive behavior and goal-oriented inspiration seem to end up being ambiguous. All humankind has a storage tank of malevolent intent towards others varying from minimally meddlesome and fleeting ideas to pure psychopathic deviant habits with no cohesive rationality. This is called the Dark Continuum. Mitigating elements functioning as accelerants and attractants to approaching the Dark Selfhood and where a person's criminal activities fall on the Dark Continuum, is what Dark Psychology calls Dark Aspect.

Dark Psychology is both the research study of criminal & deviant behavior and a conceptual framework for figuring out the possibility for evil within all people.

"Dark Psychology is not simply the dark side of our moon, yet the dark side of all moons integrated."

Do you know your dark sides, how to use them, and how to control them? Would you like to be able to recognize when someone is manipulating you? This book will help you learn about the different nuances of dark psychology and manipulation with many real-life examples and typical phrases that manipulating people use to control you and your decisions. You'll increase your self-awareness, and you'll be able to manage toxic people better to achieve a better life.

CHAPTER 19:

How to Apply Dark Psychology in Your Own Life

People use psychology within their daily lives, so why not use Dark Psychology and the tactics to protect yourself in everyday life. There are quite a few personality traits that can be very harmful if you get caught up in them. Sadists fall under this category. For instance, this personality type enjoys inflicting suffering on others, especially those who are innocent. They will even do this at the risk of costing them something. Those diagnosed as sadists feel that cruelty is a type of pleasure that is exciting and can even be sexually stimulating.

We do have to face the fact that we manipulate people and deceive people all the time. When it comes to deception, people are deceiving others daily, but they are also deceiving themselves. People often lie to gain something or to avoid something. They might not want to be punished for action, or they might want to reach a goal, and they self-deceive to get there.

Here are some examples of how people can deceive themselves:

Having a hard time studying: this is a common occurrence. When people are trying to study, they find many things that can distract them, especially cell phones and social media apps. They will find just about anything to distract them from the task at hand. These types of people seem to have a phobia of not studying long or well enough. They are afraid that they will come home with a bad grade and show how unintelligent they are. So, they take the art of self-deception and develop the idea that will help prevent them from studying. This excuse will weigh better in their mind if they do end up getting a bad grade on their test. The person's subconscious tells them that it is better for them to get bad grades for lack of studying than to study and failing and therefore having to blame their intelligence. They couldn't live with that.

Here are other ways that we regularly deceive ourselves:

- Procrastinating: People often waste time when they do not want to study or do something important. However, the main reason for procreating could be the phobia of failing, and procrastinating was just an excuse. Self-confidence can be an issue as well.

- Drinking, doing drugs, and carrying out bad habits: People often fall into bad habits, drink, or do drugs just to have something to blame if they fall again. This type of person will try to convince themselves that they could be very successful if they could stop doing drugs. When they are the ones deceiving themselves and standing in their way.

- People often hold back because life is unfair. They tell themselves that we all live in a big lie that most people believe in, but not them. It is easier to blame it on life being unfair then hold ourselves accountable for not reaching our goals.

If you realize that you have been deceiving yourself, here is a couple of things that you can do to change that.

- Remember that you are smart, and the fact that you have been able to deceive yourself reaffirms it. If you were not smart, there would have been no way that you would have been able to come up with some of those ideas.

- It is important to learn how to face your fears. If you are running from a certain trauma or not wanting to take a test, you must remind yourself that you are stronger than this and beat it.

- Lastly, once you face your fears, your self-confidence and courage will grow.

Manipulation in Our Daily Lives

Manipulation is an underhanded tactic that we are exposed to daily. Manipulators want nothing more than to get their needs met, but they will use shady methods to do so.

Those who grew up being manipulated, or being around manipulation, find it hard to determine what is going on. If you are experiencing it again, it might feel familiar. Maybe you were manipulated in a relationship, or the current relationship you are in reminds you of your childhood.

This is important because manipulation tactics break apart communication and break a person's trust. People will often find ways to manipulate the situation and play games rather than speaking honestly about what is going on. However, others value communication only to manipulate the situation to reveal the other person's weaknesses so that they can be in control. These types of people often do this in conversation. They have no concern with listening to others talk about anything about themselves. And they are not there to help those people get through whatever it is that they are going through. It is all about dominance in this case, and that's it.

Here are some of the tactics that can be used on an everyday basis:

Some of the common techniques that we can experience are:

- **Lying**: White lies, untruths, partial or half-truths, exaggerations, and stretching the truth.

- **Love Flooding**: Through endless compliments, affection, or through what is known as buttering someone up.

- **Love Denial**: Telling someone that they do not love you and withhold your love or affection from them until you get what you want.

- **Withdrawal**: Through avoiding the person altogether or giving them the silent treatment.

- **Choice Restriction**: Giving people options that distract them from the one you don't want them to make.

- **Reverse Psychology**: Trying to get a person to do the exact opposite of what you want them to do to motivate them to do the direct opposite, which is what you wanted them to do in the first place.

- **Being Condescendingly Sarcastic or Having a Patronizing Tone**: To be fair, we are all guilty of doing this once in a while. But those who are manipulating us in conversation are doing this consistently. They mocked you; their tone indicates that you are a child, and they belittle you with their words.

- **Speaking in Universal Statement or Generalizations**: The manipulator will take the statement and make it untrue by grossly making it bigger. Generalizations are afforded to those who a part of a group of things. A universal statement is more personal.

Example: of Universal Example: You always say things like that.

Example of Generalization: Therapists always act like that.

- **Luring and Then Playing Innocent**: We, or someone we know, are good at pushing our loved ones' buttons. However, when a manipulator tries to push their spouse's buttons and then act like they have no idea what happened. They automatically get the reaction they were after. This is when their partner needs to pay close attention to what they are doing. Those who are abusive will keep doing this again and again until their spouse will start wondering if they are crazy.

- **Bullying**: This is one of the easiest forms of manipulation to recognize. For example, your spouse asks you to clean the kitchen. You don't want to, but the look they are giving you indicates that you better clean it or else. You tell them sure, but they just used a form of violence to get you to do what they wanted. Later they could have told you that you could have said no, but you knew you couldn't. It is important to note that if you fear that you cannot say no if your relationship without fearing for your safety, then you need to leave the relationship.

- **Using Your Heart Against You**: Your spouse finds a stray kitten and wants to bring it home. The logical thing to do would be to discuss being able to house and afford the cat. But instead, they take the manipulative approach. Their ultimate goal is to make you feel bad about not being able to take care of the animal. Don't let anyone, even your spouse, make you feel that you cannot make the best choice for you. You do not have to take care of the kitten if you don't want to. Bottom line. Meet their manipulations with reasonable alternatives.

- **"If you love me, you would do this"**: This one is so hard because it challenges how you feel about your spouse. They are asking you to prove your love for them by giving them what they want from you, making you feel guilt and shame. The thing you can do in this instance is to stop it altogether. You can tell your spouse that you love them without having to go to the store. If they wanted, you to go they could just ask.

- **Emotional Blackmail**: This is ugly and dangerous. The idea that someone will harm themselves if you leave them is harmful at the core. They are using guilt, fear, and shame to keep having power over you. Remember that no one's total well-being is your responsibility alone. You have to tell yourself not to fall for it. This will always be a manipulation tactic. However, you can tell them that if they are feeling like they are going to harm themselves that you will call an ambulance to help them.

- **Neediness when it's Convenient**: Has your spouse started to feel sick or upset when they didn't get what they wanted? This is a direct form of manipulation. For instance, they don't want to go somewhere with you and have a panic attack, that you have to help them through, so that they don't have to go at all. This is not healthy at all, and if this persists, you should think about ending the relationship.

- **They Are Calm in Bad Situations:** When someone gets hurt, or their conflict, somebody dies, your spouse always seems to not react with any feeling. They are always calm. This type of manipulation makes you think that perhaps how you are reacting is a bit much. Maybe your emotions are a little bit out of control. This is a controlling mechanism because no one should be able to tell you how to feel. This might seem like they are questioning your mental health and maturity level, and you find yourself looking to them and how to respond in certain situations. If this something that happens often and you see that you keep falling for it, you might need to go and see a therapist. This way, they can help you work on your emotional responses and find your true feelings again. This manipulation method can be very damaging to your psyche. At the moment, learn to trust your gut. It will not steer you wrong.

- **Everything is a Joke:** This is a two-part manipulation tactic. Your spouse will say hurtful things about you, and then when you get upset, they get upset because you can't take a joke. Other times they will joke about you in front of others, and if you don't respond positively, you are again ruining the fun. This is a way to put you down continuously without having to take responsibility for it. Remember that you are not ruining the fun here, but you have to stand up for yourself.

CHAPTER 20:

Benefits in Your Life with Guided Meditation Exercises

You are most likely here right now because you have heard amazing, life-changing aspects meditation can bring to your life. Whether you are looking to improve your mental health, performance, physical health, or better your relationship with yourself or others, meditation could be the perfect practice for you.

Mental Health Benefits

Unfortunately, many individuals suffer from mental health issues. Whether you are dealing with anxiety, depression, or something along those lines, meditation can help place you in a better mindset when practiced regularly.

Decrease Depression

In a study done in Belgium, four-hundred students were placed in an in-class mindfulness program to see if it could reduce their stress, anxiety, and depression. It was found that six months later, the students who practiced were less likely to develop depression-like symptoms. It was found that mindfulness meditation could potentially be just as effective as an antidepressant drug! In another study, women going through a high-risk pregnancy were asked to participate in a mindfulness yoga exercise for ten weeks. After the time passed, there was a significant reduction in the symptoms often caused by depression. On top of the benefit of less depression, the mothers also showed signs of having a more intense bond with their child while it was still in the womb.

Reduce Anxiety and Depression

In general, meditation may be best known for the mental health benefits of reducing the symptoms associated with anxiety and depression. It was found that through meditation, individuals who practiced meditation such as Vipassana or "Open Monitoring Meditation" were able to reduce the grey-matter density in their brains. This grey-matter is related to stress and anxiety. When individuals practice meditation, it helps create an environment where they can live moment to moment rather than getting stuck in one situation. While practicing meditation, the positive mindset may be able to help regulate anxiety and mood disorders that are associated with panic disorders. There was one article published in the American Journal of Psychiatry based around twenty-two different patients who had panic or anxiety disorders. After three months of relaxation and meditation, twenty of the twenty-two were able to reduce the effects of their panic and anxiety.

Performance Benefits

When you can relax, you would be amazed at how much better your brain will function. By letting go of stress, you leave room for positive thoughts in your head and will be able to make better decisions for yourself. It's a win-win situation when you can improve your mood and your performance simply from meditation.

Better Decision Making

A study done at UCLA found that individuals who practiced meditation for a long time had a larger amount of gyrification in the brain. This is the "folding" along the cortex, which is directly related to processing information faster. Compared to individuals who do not practice meditation, it was found that meditators could form memories easier, make quicker decisions, and process information at a higher rate overall.

Improve Focus and Attention

Another study performed at the University of California suggested that subjects can increase their focus on tasks through meditation, especially ones that are boring and repetitive. It was found that even after only twenty minutes of meditation practice, individuals can increase their cognitive skills ten times better compared to those who do not practice mindfulness.

Along the same lines, it's believed that meditation may help manage those who have ADHD, or attention deficit hyperactivity disorder. There was a study performed on fifty adults who had ADHD. The group was placed through mindfulness-based cognitive therapy to see how it would affect their ADHD. In the end, it was found that these individuals were able to act with awareness while reducing both their impulsivity and hyperactivity. Overall, they were able to improve their inattention.

Relieve Pain

It has been said that meditation could potentially relieve pain better when compared to morphine. This may be possible since pain is subjective. There was a study done on thirteen Zen masters compared to thirteen non-practitioners. These individuals were exposed to painful heat while having their brain activity watched. The Zen masters reported less pain, and the neurological output reported less pain as well. This goes to show that pain truly is a mental aspect.

Along the same lines, mindfulness training could also help patients who have been diagnosed with Fibromyalgia. In one study, eleven patients went through eight weeks of mindfulness training. At the end of the study, these individuals' overall health improved, and reported more good days than bad.

Avoid Multitasking Too Often

While multitasking can seem like a good skill to have at some points, it's also an excellent way to become overwhelmed and stressed out. Unfortunately, multitasking can be very dangerous to your productivity. When you ask your brain to switch gears between activities, this often can produce distractions from your work being done. A study was performed on students at the University of Arizona and the University of Washington. These people were placed through eight weeks of mindfulness meditation. During this time, the students had to perform a stressful test demonstrating multitasking before and after the training. It was shown that those who practiced meditation could increase their memory and lower their stress while multitasking.

Physical Benefits

While mental improvements are fantastic benefits of meditation, physical benefits can help motivate individuals to begin meditation. Unfortunately, the standard of health is to turn to medication. If you are an individual who hates popping pills for every issue you have; meditation may be just what you need to help improve your health.

Reduce Risk of Stroke and Heart Disease

It has been found that heart disease is one of the world's top killers compared to other illnesses. Through meditation, you could lower your risk of both heart disease and stroke. There was a study done in 2012 for a group of two hundred high-risk people.

These individuals were asked to take a class on health, exercise, or take a class on meditation. Over the next five years, it was found that the individuals who chose meditation were able to reduce their risk of death, stroke, and heart attacks by almost half!

Reduce High Blood Pressure

In a clinical study based around meditation, it was also found that certain Zen meditations such as Zazen, can lower both stress and high blood pressures. It's believed that relaxation response techniques could lower blood pressure levels after three short months of practicing. Through meditation, individuals had less need for medication for their blood pressure! This could be because, when we relax, it helps open your blood vessels through nitric oxide formation.

Live a Longer Life

When you get rid of stress in your life, you may be amazed at how much more energetic and healthier you feel. While the research hasn't been drawn to a conclusion yet, some studies suggest meditation could affect our cells' telomere length. Telomeres are in charge of how our cells age. When there is less cognitive stress, it helps maintain telomere and other hormonal factors.

Relationship Benefits

Some people are looking for a little bit more peace in your life. In the world we live in today, times can be very trying. There are constant deadlines, bills to pay, people to deal with, but now is the time to look at stressors in your life under a different life. Through meditation, you can become a more caring and empathetic individual to create a more peaceful life for yourself.

Improve Positive Relationships and Empathy

When we undergo stressful situations with obnoxious people, it can be very trying to remain empathetic. There is a Buddhist tradition of practicing loving-kindness meditation that may help foster a sense of care toward all living things. Through meditation, you'll be able to boost the way you read facial expressions and gain the ability to empathize with others. When you have a loving attitude toward yourself and others, this helps develop a positive relationship with them and a sense of self-acceptance.

Decrease Feelings of Loneliness

Many people are not okay with being alone. Often, we try to fill our time with activities so that we are never alone with ourselves. The truth is, it can be healthy to spend some time with yourself so that you can self-reflect on your life choices. In a study published in Brain, Behavior, and Immunity, it was proven that after thirty minutes of meditation per day, it reduced individuals' sense of loneliness while reducing the risks of premature death, depression, and perhaps even Alzheimer's.

Besides feeling less lonely, meditation also opens up new doors to feeling a positive connection to yourself. When you love yourself, and you are happy with your own company, you may spend a lot less time on negative thoughts and feelings of self-doubt; both of which can lead to self-caused stress.

Affirmations are "I" statements that help to reiterate an important point. They will help guide you in establishing positive thoughts and a healthy pattern of thinking. It can be easy to get into the habit of telling ourselves negative affirmations. These might include "I am not good enough" or "I am ugly."

Too much thinking that involves this kind of idea will lead you to feel as though you are not successful. These affirmations will take you through the right pattern of thinking to feel positive and have a mindset geared toward fulfilling your biggest fantasies.

Repeat these to yourself daily to retrain your brain. Write them down and leave notes around your house. Repeat them more than once and write them down to reiterate the overall message of these positive affirmations.

Breathe in through your nose and out of your mouth right before reading them to clear your mind and relax your body. Read them in a calm place so you can focus on the message the most.

CHAPTER 21:

Speed Reading People

What Is Speeding People?

Ignite the Art of Reading People through Your Super Senses

If you want to read people, you have to don the garment of a psychiatrist who can interpret cues that are verbal and nonverbal. You need to observe beyond people's masks into their real selves. You may not get the entire picture of anybody through logic alone.

You have to surrender to their critical forms of information to interpret the essential nonverbal perceptive cues individuals exude. To achieve this feat, you need to be eager to surrender emotional baggage like ego clashes or old resentments and any preconceptions that can prevent you from making out the person. It is crucial, as well, for you to obtain information without bias and continue to be impartial without twisting it.

In the process of reading a colleague, your boss, or partner for you to understand them accurately, some walls need to come down, and you need to surrender biases. You need to be ready to let go of limiting, old ideas as far as intellect is concerned.

Those who read other people well are taught to comprehend the hidden. They have discovered how they will draw on 'super-sense' to take a profound observation beyond where you usually steer your focus when you attempt to hack into transformative awareness.

Examine cues of body language

When you read the cues of body language, you have to surrender the focus by releasing your struggle to understand the hidden signals of body language. Never get analytical or overtly intense. Stay fluid and relaxed. Observe by sitting back comfortably.

Focus on appearance

When you are reading other people, take note of what they are wearing. Are they putting on well-shined shoes and a power suit? The indication for success is when someone deck out decently. For someone wearing a T-shirt and jeans may be an indicator of that person being comfortable with casual. It may be a signal of a seductive choice when someone wears a tight top with cleavage. A pendant like Buddha or cross may indicate spiritual values.

Notice Posture

Postures are an essential aspect of reading people. It's a sign of confident when people's head is held high. Or you can get an indication of low self-esteem when they cower or they walk irresolutely. You can also get a sign of a big ego when they have a puffed-out chest and swagger.

Pay attention to physical movements

When you read others, look out for their distance and learning. In general, people bend forward at those they like and keep a distance from others. When people cross their arms and legs, you can see signs of anger, self-protection, or defensiveness. It is an indication that people are hiding something when they hide their hands by placing them in their pockets, laps, or place them behind them. With cuticle picking or lip biting, you will get a sign of people attempting to calm themselves in a difficult circumstance or under pressure.

Read facial expression

Our faces provide the outline for our emotions. Profound frown lines indicate over-thinking or worry. The smile lines of delight are crow's feet; pursed lips are a signal of contempt, anger, or bitterness. While teeth grinding and clenched jaw are indicators of tension.

Take note of your intuition

It is possible to tune into someone ahead of their words and body language. Though not what your head says, what your gut feels is intuition. Instead of logic, intuition is your perception of nonverbal information through images. If you are in the process of understanding a person, their outer trappings are insignificant, and it is only who the person is what counts. To reveal a richer story, intuition gives the power to distinguish beyond the obvious to tell a richer story.

You need to watch out for these checklists cues of intuition:

Respect your gut feelings

Pay attention to the voices of your gut, in particular when connecting with someone for the first time. This automatic rejoinder happens out of impulse. Gut feelings are as a result of if you are tensed up or at ease. As a cardinal response, gut feelings occur in an instant. They are meters of your inner truth that relay to you if you should trust someone.

Goosebumps feelings

Pleasant, intuitive shivers are goosebumps. They happen when something strikes a chord in us in connection with our resonance to individuals that inspire or move us. Also, goosebumps occur in the course of going through déjà-vu and when you have never met someone before but still recognize them.

Listen to sparkles of insight

During a conversation with people, you may be impressed by those who come quickly. Watch out and stay alert. Or else, you might fail to spot it. For most of us, this crucial awareness is lost because of the inclination to move onto the next idea.

Look for insightful empathy

This cue happens when you have a passionate type of empathy through someone's real emotions and symptoms within your body. So, while reading people, note whether you had pain on your back when it wasn't there before or if you are upset or depressed following a mind-numbing conference. To determine if empathy is at play, get feedback.

Discern emotional power

The vibe we radiate and the remarkable demonstration of our energy are emotions. It is with an intuition that we procure these emotions. You will be happy to be around them for some people because they enhance your vitality and mood. Others tend to be draining; get away from them is what you want. Though it is undetectable, you can feel this 'subtle energy' feet or inches from the body. It's called *chi* in Chinese medicine, an essential healthy vitality.

Be aware of the presence of people

Though not substantially similar to our behavior or words, the accustomed energy we discharge is when we sense the people's presence. It is typical of a rain cloud or the sun that borders around our emotional atmosphere. In reading people, take note of if you get attraction by their presence or retreating due to the willies you are getting.

Watch people's eyes

Humans' eyes convey compelling forces. As the eyes cast off an electromagnetic signal, according to studies, the brain does the same. When you watch people's eyes, you will know if they are tranquil, sexy, mean, angry, or caring. You will also have the ability to determine if a person wants intimacy in their eyes, or their eyes can give signs that they are comfortable. Even in their eyes, you will know whether they appear to be hiding or guarded.

Observe the feel of a hug, handshake, or touch

Most of us shake emotional energy, similar to an electrical flow during physical contact. You can ask yourself if a hug or handshake feels comfortable, warm, or confident. Or if it is repulsive so much that you wish to withdraw. You can know the sign of anxiety with someone's hand clammy or limp to suggest being timid or non-committal.

Listen to the tone of laugh and voice

Our voice's volume and tone are capable of telling a lot about our emotions. Vibration is a result of sound frequencies. Notice how people's pitch of voice affects you in the course of reading them. Envisage if the tone is snippy, abrasive, and whiny or if their tone feels soothing.

To read, people can be hard sometimes. It takes practice and courage. However, once you are past that, you will gain a significant advantage. Not only will you survive, but you will also thrive in all your relationships with others. People will approach you. Opportunities will come to you. And some people will want to be like you.

CHAPTER 22:

Advanced Human Psychology You Need to Know

What Motivates People

Manipulation and persuasion are huge topics in this guidebook. Therefore, it is essential to learn what motivates people. When you learn what motivates people, you gain the knowledge necessary to make people feel motivated to do what you want. Motivating others to do what you want is the cornerstone of manipulation and persuasion. Of course, we cover how to use manipulation and persuasion. First, we must make it clear how manipulation and persuasion can work. What causes people to want to do things? How can you use this knowledge for your purposes?

A single force does not always cause motivation. It is often a combination of forces that act upon a person, driving them to want to do something.

Reward Philosophy

Motivation relies on the fact that humans seek rewards for what they do. People don't do things that offer them no reward of any kind. They want some sort of return for their time, energy, and effort. This is why we go to jobs that we don't exactly enjoy, and tolerate bosses or co-workers who drive us crazy because we get paid and can survive due to our effort. We are motivated to work because it provides us with the sustenance that we need to continue to survive in our society.

Ivan Pavlov's work with dogs in the 1890s confirms this reward theory. Pavlovian conditioning is now the cornerstone of modern psychology because it shed so much light on what motivates animals, including people. In Pavlov's work, dogs would salivate when he entered the room because they expected a reward of food. They had formed an association between him and food. They were also willing to perform tricks and actions for him when they anticipated a food reward. Subsequent studies with rats and human subjects have proved that this conditioning works. A reward triggers an action. Sometimes this action is unintentional or unconditioned. We'll revisit this concept shortly because unconditioned responses tie into motivating people in covert ways. You can use it to essentially "train" a person to do what you want.

Back to motivation. To be covert, you can use conditioning, or you can pretend to "unintentionally" open the doors for someone to get what they want by doing what you want. You don't' have to be obvious about offering someone something that they want. Instead, make them see by themselves that they can get what they want by pleasing you or doing something for you.

Rewards need to equal the amount of effort that someone perceives they will have to put into something. Make sure to offer something big for big things and something small for small things. It is acceptable to bargain with a person to agree on a reward that they are happy with. If you want to be more covert, it is best to observe the person and figure out what he wants.

Another powerful secret: People are highly motivated to escape ugly emotions, such as guilt or shame. If you use guilt to your advantage, you can make someone want to do something because they will feel bad if they don't. No one wants to feel bad. You can use guilt to motivate people. Either point out how they will hurt you or make them feel that they can gain redemption for something bad that they did in the past to someone else by acting now. Churches use this concept by asking for tithes from people to repent for their sins and the fact that Jesus Christ died on the cross for their sins. Acting like someone is hurting you by doing something can make them want to stop doing it because they feel guilty about it.

Conditioning

It is possible to train people to do what you want. You can motivate people by creating an unconditioned response. This goes back to the Pavlovian conditioning that you want to make someone associate you with a reward. You don't always have to deliver this reward; you just need to create an association. The anticipation of it based on past rewards is sufficient to get people motivated.

Pavlov discovered that his dogs would salivate even when they saw the lab assistant, who typically didn't bring food. They would also salivate whenever they saw Pavlov, regardless of whether or not he was bearing food. When he started experimenting with a bell, he learned that the dogs would salivate because they associated the bell's sound with getting food. Presenting two stimuli close together in timing helped create these responses, or in other words, conditioned the dogs.

The great thing about conditioning is that it can be subtle, however. You can train someone to expect something pleasurable when they do something without making it obvious. I'll illustrate this with a few examples to make the concept clear.

So, here's another aspect of conditioning that makes you more covert. You can become a neutral stimulus. In Pavlovian conditioning, a stimulus elicits a response. A neutral stimulus causes a response, even though that stimulus never offers a reward. You can make people respond to your very presence, even if you don't directly do anything. You do this by creating associations in people's brains between you and some sort of reward. You want to make people feel positively toward you, so you want to strive to create a powerful association between you and a good reward. Here's a great example of how you can become a neutral stimulus and elicit the response that you desire. You have a lazy roommate who never wants to do dishes. One day, she does the dishes, so you play a song that she likes as she does it. She will associate great music with doing dishes. From now on, she'll want to do dishes more. The minute you put on the song; she will go do dishes. You have created a conditioned response in her. She responds to her favorite song by doing dishes. This is essentially training someone, like a dog.

Convenience

People hate expending too much effort. They won't do it if they think that the reward is not sufficient to compensate them. The most basic illustration of this concept is shopping. If you try to sell something that is priced at more than its dollar worth, then people most likely won't buy it. You want to make sure that people perceive that their effort is worth the reward they will receive.

You can also present a good reward. The better the reward, the more likely people will go the extra mile.

Confirmation Bias

Here is a little habit most people have that you can certainly use to your advantage in dark psychology. This is called confirmation bias. It's where people pick and choose evidence from a stimulus, they see to confirm the beliefs or prejudices that they already hold. People will choose to believe something, then search for confirmation in the world around them. They will also ignore or reject information that goes against their bias. It is very hard to change someone's mind. They usually like to stick to their own beliefs and ideas with little variation. They hate being challenged or told that they're wrong, and they will find ways to dispute all evidence that proves them wrong.

Competition

You must understand that people are in constant competition. People may be friends, but even friends want to beat each other. Everyone vies for the best. Therefore, competition is an underlying current in all relationships. It can rip friendships apart.

Jealousy is one of the nastiest emotions out there. People hate to feel jealous. Yet, it is easy for many people to feel this emotion spark up. You can play on the envy of others to motivate people to go after things that others have. You can also use envy to turn friends against each other. Making people jealous of you can elevate your status as a person.

Attribution Error

For instance, a woman who has had many sexual partners might be proud of her conquests. Still, she may call another woman with an equal number of partners a "slut." She may assume that any woman who sleeps with a lot of men has emotional issues and daddy issues and, as a result, feels the need to sleep around. She doesn't attribute her own sexual experience to these internal factors, however.

Or a person might think that others who litter are just lazy good-for-nothings who don't care about the environment. Still, when he accidentally drops a cup when his arms are full of trash, and it rolls away in the breeze, he shrugs and figures that he tried his best to get all of the trash in the wastebasket.

People don't like to think lowly of themselves, and they tend to excuse their actions, but they hold others to more exacting standards. This bias causes people to judge others more harshly than they judge themselves. The saying that we are our own harshest critics is often untrue. Rather, we judge others more harshly than ourselves.

You can use this bias to break down others' self-esteem and make them feel that everything they do is their fault. It is one of the keys to emotional abuse. It is also a great way to use psychological warfare to beat on someone who makes a mistake. You can get a whole office to believe that the person who made a simple mistake doesn't care about the company's welfare and is inefficient, lazy, and incompetent.

Liking

Liking is a key part of getting ahead in the world. Taken from Cialdini's Principles of Influence, this concept can gain you lots of influence over others. If you appear well-liked and popular, then more and more people will like you. But people will tend to avoid you if they notice that you have no friends. This is why it can be hard to make new friends if you relocate to a different city, as people won't want to approach you if you are all alone.

Therefore, you can get ahead in life by not being alone. Appear liked. This makes others want to like you and talk to you. You can gain a lot of respect and favor. People will be more likely to do what you want, respect you, and trust you if you appear to be liked by many people. This is why people place such huge importance on social media likes. It gives the illusion of popularity.

What People Care About

People have a list of things that they hold very dear. When these things are attacked, people tend to get very defensive. You can gain a lot of power over someone by finding out what he cares about so passionately.

Most people can only be pushed so far. Understanding someone's limits can be very helpful when you are trying.

CHAPTER 23:

How to Stop Procrastinating and Change Habits

It is true that overthinking leads to procrastination, right? Well, it's also true that procrastination leads to overthinking. Procrastination will harm your productivity. Pushing things to a sooner time only increases your anxiety. You will fill your mind with constant worry since you are never sure whether you will complete a particular task or not. Bearing this in mind, it is not surprising that you will find yourself overthinking because you have developed a habit of procrastinating.

About one-fifth of adults procrastinate. Simply put, procrastination refers to the notion of postponing making decisions. Instead of doing something right away, you decide to do it soon. Unfortunately, this takes a toll on you as it reduces productivity, poor mental health, increased worry, stress, etc.

Why Do People Procrastinate?

Have you ever stopped to question yourself why you keep procrastinating even though you know very well that it harms your well-being? Indeed, procrastination can increase anxiety simply because you will always struggle to get things done. What's more, you will worry too much about the possibility of failing to accomplish your goals due to wasted time. But why do people procrastinate even though they know what needs to be done?

Undeniably, before dealing with a problem, you have to identify its root cause. Therefore, you must comprehend the main reasons that push people to procrastinate.

Fear of Failure

One of the main reasons why people procrastinate is because they fear failing. When one has a gut feeling that they will not do something successfully, it increases the likelihood of postponing their actions. You ought to understand that there is an inherent guarantee that you will not fail because you failed to take action. When you fail to take action, procrastination comes in to comfort you. It protects you from the possibility of failing. To overcome your fear of failure, you should bear in mind that failing is not the end of everything. It is not fatal. Mistakes are there to help you find another route towards success. This means that failing is part of success. You must train yourself to develop a mindset where you believe that not taking any action is the worst thing that you can do. It's better to try and fail than simply do nothing.

Excessive Perfectionism

Perfectionism will also push you to procrastinate. Individuals who consider themselves perfectionists will want to postpone things simply because they believe they will not do certain things perfectly. Having this attitude is that it creates worry since one will not be sure whether they can meet the high-quality standards that they have set for themselves.

The problem with being a perfectionist is that you end up creating unrealistic expectations for yourself. Accordingly, you will feel that it's better to do nothing because you're not sure of your abilities.

Low Energy Levels

Of course, if you don't have the energy to do something now, there is a good chance that you will want to do it soon. Normally, this is an excuse that is used by individuals with unhealthy lifestyles. They lack the vital energy that is required to attend to their day to day routines.

As a solution to this problem, people should strive to be healthy by engaging in physical activity. A healthier lifestyle will boost your productivity since you will enhance your physical and mental health. Ultimately, you will find it easy to make decisions without procrastinating.

Lack of Focus

Your lack of focus will often push you to procrastinate. This is because you don't have a direction to follow when working towards achieving your goals. Failure to have a purpose in life will only make you feel less motivated. The lack of focus affects how you dispel your energy since you will want to do just anything that keeps your mind engaged. You will find that you have wasted time doing something that adds little or no value to your life. The worst thing is that you end up going to bed feeling guilty about your poor time management. The following morning, the process repeats itself and the cycle continues. Before you know it, you are depressed and lost in your world.

To overcome this challenge, it is important to set achievable short term and long-term goals. These can be hourly, daily, weekly or monthly goals. By achieving these goals, you will motivate yourself to work harder towards achieving other larger goals. When setting goals, remember to raise the bar as this ensures that you have something to work hard for. Don't just set goals for the sake of it. Set goals to achieve them.

Disconnect From Your Future Self

You might be tempted to procrastinate because there is a disconnect between your present and your future self. A good example of this is being advised to eat healthier. Most people will not heed their doctor's recommendations because what they eat now will not directly affect them from the word go. The foods you eat today will affect you more so in the long run.

Accordingly, such a disconnect from the future influences people to procrastinate and choose to do something sooner instead of now. The point here is that people will worry less about their present selves. Moreover, they will want the future self to worry about what will happen in the future. So, your present self-will rarely worries about the consequences of failing to complete a certain task today.

Distractions

Modern-day distractions can also deter you from working productively. In today's world, you will be distracted by emails, social media, text messages, people, etc. Instead of working on a task that you were commissioned to do, you find yourself wasting a lot of time on Facebook, Twitter, Instagram, etc. Before you know it, you have wasted an hour or two on these social media pages. Distractions from the digital world will affect your productivity. In extreme cases, it will lead to stress. This is because you will still have several pending tasks on your to-do list when you finish the workday. Sometimes this might mean that you will need to work overtime to compensate for the time lost. Constantly working overtime is a sign of poor time management.

Avoid this from happening by using your time wisely. Eliminate these distractions by choosing to disconnect yourself from the digital world for some time. After all, there is nothing that you will lose by muting your phone for a couple of hours before checking it.

Negative Effects of Procrastination on Your Life

No one is a stranger to procrastination. At one point in your life, you must have postponed doing something now with the idea of doing it soon. Some people might be less susceptible to procrastination. They can quickly identify that they are procrastinating too much and make the necessary changes. However, others fail to recognize that they are developing a bad habit that could prevent them from reaching their goals. Procrastination can destroy your life in many ways. It's not just about killing time or failing to do certain things immediately. Your life can take a drastic turn that you never anticipated. The following are some effects of procrastination that you ought to be aware of.

Losing Precious Time

When pushing things to attend to them soon, we end up wasting a lot of time. How many hours do you think you have wasted by procrastinating? Say you postpone doing a certain task during your normal workdays. By the end of the week, there is little that you will have achieved. The worst thing about this is that you will have lost precious time. What's more, the time lost cannot be recovered. You'll only live regretting and wishing that you did things on time. A major problem arises when procrastination becomes a habit. The bitter truth is that you will only realize weeks, months, or years after that time has gone, and there is nothing you have done to change your life for the better. Undeniably, any amount of time lost is a lot of time wasted.

You Will Fail to Achieve Your Goals

We work with a rebellious mind. The moment your mind notices that you want to change something in your life, it goes against it. It is for this reason that we often find it difficult to maintain routines. The mind has a mind of its own, and it yearns to control itself. So, when you ponder that you should set goals in your life, your mind will reject such change. As a result, you will find it easy to procrastinate working on the things that you have listed as your goals.

Have you ever wondered how so many people know what to do when it comes to losing weight, but few do what needs to be done? It's all because of the rebellious mind and our inclination to procrastinate. The more you procrastinate, the more you push your goals away from you. Your life will never be fulfilling if there is nothing worth achieving.

Negative Impact on Your Career

Your career will heavily depend on your performance. By working towards meeting your goals and your business' goals, there is a good chance that you will succeed in what you do. The company where you work has its own goals. Your productivity is required to make sure that the company meets them. If you are a procrastinator, it becomes difficult to attain these goals. This means that you will be sacrificing your career simply because you cannot make desirable actions to act immediately. Think about it this way, there is a lot that you will miss out on, including promotions and salary raises. When things get out of hand, there is a higher chance that you will lose your job. Therefore, failure to do something about procrastination will be detrimental to your life and your career.

Lower Self-Esteem

One of the reasons why you will push things to a future time is because of low self-esteem. Maybe you are not sure about how to handle a certain assignment. Therefore, you might want to procrastinate so that you can handle it only when you feel ready. What you fail to realize is that procrastination only worsens things as it lowers your self-esteem further. The mere fact that you can't get things done in time will destroy the little self-esteem that you may have in you. Expect your mind to be overflowing with thoughts of self-doubt. Eventually, this leads to stress and anxiety.

Poor Decision Making

Once you procrastinate, there is a high chance that you will make poor decisions because you will be in a race against time. You will not be thinking clearly. Some of your decisions will require you to think and act fast because of your lack of time. If you hadn't procrastinated in the first place, you wouldn't need to make these decisions at such a rapid rate.

CHAPTER 24:

How to Use Psychological Manipulation Techniques to Make Your Work and Life Better

Have you ever noticed that the most successful people are also the most persuasive? In the workplace, it is rarely the aggressive bossy people that rise to the top. Great leaders have a knack for making other people feel better about themselves and achieve better results. Use the following techniques to become a better manipulator both at work and at home.

Inspire Confidence

Do you give compliments regularly? Are you quick to praise people when they achieve their goals? If not, then why not? A few words can go a long way to boost someone's confidence. Make sure you tell people when they have done a good job and encourage them to greater things.

Once you master this technique and feel comfortable giving praise, this will spill over into your personal life. If your partner looks sensational, then tell them! If your kids have done well at school, then reward them with your praise. Only give sincere compliments and do not use them to play people. If you are using manipulation to avoid tasks at work, you will soon get a reputation for using people.

Repetition

Many people believe that passion alone can make an idea stand out amid a sea of other ideas. This is not true and successful people realize that the key to standing out in society's information overload is repetition. We have all developed filters to protect us from the bombardment of information in this media-led world and need to hear something multiple times before it sinks in. If you have a great idea and voice it to someone, make sure you follow up with a written version.

Deliver Your Message in Context

We are often tempted to make ourselves look more intelligent by using technical jargon or abstract references. You will achieve much better results if you tune into your audience's frame of mind. Avoid non-specific terms. If you have an idea to make things "easier to use" or "better and quicker," then state how much easier or how much better and quicker.

Personalize Your Message

Statements of fact can often be bland and uninteresting. If you can personalize your speech you have a greater impact on your audience. This is a great tool at work. If you are approaching someone creative then tailor your speech to reflect this. This technique will also help your social life. Whenever you meet new people, try and do a bit of homework, so you know more about them.

Use Your Contacts

Everyone is more open to people who they believe have mutual associations. Your connections can help you progress and providing you don't abuse their influence, they can aid your progress at work. Your credibility can rise with the relevance of your contacts and friends.

Use Visualization Techniques

Have you noticed that the most successful sales pitches have a strong visual element? Picture Apples Steve Jobs and you can visualize the stage and the graphics that he used to get his message across. Even his clothes became part of the whole message that Apple was trying to convey. Not everyone will comprehend what you see in your mind's eye, especially if they have less knowledge in the domain you represent.

Social Media

Do you use social media to its full potential? Are you prepared to invest time and energy in your online connections? If not, then you are missing a huge opportunity. The potential to reach thousands of people who can help you in your career is invaluable.

Potential investors or customers are all waiting for you to tell your story or promote your product. Social media allows you to solicit ideas from a huge audience, all with the click of a mouse. The power of a "like button" is not to be ignored! The evidence of thousands of positive affirmations will only serve to amplify your voice and make more people listen.

Your social life can also thrive online. Groups of like-minded people are all out there waiting for you to join them. Maybe you have a passion for sailing or extreme sports but aren't sure of the facilities near you. Facebook is a great place to start looking for groups in your area, reach out, and connect. Use Twitter and Instagram to help your dating life if you are looking for love! Providing you take precautions and always meet for the first time in public you can meet some interesting people!

Social media can also be a brutal place, and you must monitor your settings. Before you join a group, make sure they can only see the information you are comfortable with.

Listen Intently

If you want to get someone to like you, the best way is to let them talk about themselves. Adopt a relaxed posture and allow them to tell you all about themselves. Show genuine interest and ask pertinent questions as you listen.

- What is the common factor all these questions have?

- "That is fascinating, how did you manage that?"

- "Interesting, do you have any examples of what you mean?"

- "Your knowledge about… Is amazing, what do you think about…?"

They are all questions that elicit a response. This shows the speaker that you are not just listening, but you have a genuine interest in what they say. You also allow the speaker to expand the conversation, which creates a bond between the two of you. They will see you as an ally and a person they can trust.

CHAPTER 25:

How Dark Psychology Works

As you proceed via future manuscripts broadening this construct, this author will explain one of the essential principles. The following are six tenets necessary to realize Dark Psychology as adheres to: ultimately. Dark Psychology is a global part of the human condition. All societies, societies, and individuals that reside in them keep this facet of human health. The most kindhearted individuals understood have this realm of wickedness, yet never act on it and have lower violent ideas and sensations.

1. It is the study of the human condition related to individuals' thoughts, feelings, and assumptions connected to this inherent potential to prey upon others devoid of apparent, definite reasons. Considered that all behavior is purposive, goal-oriented, and conceptualized using modus operandi, Dark Psychology puts forth the idea the nearer an individual attracts to the "black hole" of beautiful wickedness, the less most likely he/she has a purpose in inspirations. Although this writer presumes beautiful evil is never gotten to, Dark Psychology thinks some come close because it is infinite.

2. The background is loaded with instances of this unexposed propensity to disclose itself as active, harmful habits. Modern psychiatry and also psychology define the psychotic as a predator lacking remorse for his activities. Dark Psychology says there is a continuum of intensity ranging from thoughts and sensations of physical violence to extreme victimization and physical abuse without a practical objective or inspiration.

3. On this continuity, the severity of the Dark Psychology is not considered less or even more grievous by the actions of victimization, however stories out a variety of inhumanity. A straightforward picture would be contrasting Ted Bundy and also Jeffrey Dahmer. Both were severe psychos as well as horrendous in their actions. The difference is Dahmer committed his godawful murders for his delusional demand for friendship. In contrast, Ted Bundy murdered, and also sadistically brought upon discomfort out of great demented wickedness. Both would be greater on the Dark Continuum. Yet, one, Jeffrey Dahmer, can be better recognized using his psychotic hopeless requirement to be enjoyed.

4. Dark Psychology thinks all people have the potential for physical violence. This potential is innate in all people, and different interior and external variables, raise the probability for this possibility to show up right into unstable habits. These habits are predatory, as well as at times; they can function without factor. Dark Psychology assumes the predator-prey vibrant becomes misshaped by human beings. Dark Psychology is entirely a human sensation and is also shared by nothing else living animal. Physical violence and even chaos may exist in various other living organisms, but humankind is the only varieties that can do so without purpose.

5. An understanding of the underlying reasons and triggers of Dark Psychology would certainly better allow the culture to recognize, identify, and perhaps reduce the dangers inherent in its influence. Discovering the ideas of Dark Psychology serves a double beneficial feature. Initially, accepting most of us have this possibility for evil allows those with this expertise to reduce the probability of it erupting. Second of all, comprehending the tenets of Dark Psychology fits our original transformative objective for struggling to make it through.

This author's goal is to enlighten others by enhancing their self-awareness, developing a standard change of their truth for the better, and motivating those to tell others to endeavor upon finding out to minimize the possibility of succumbing to those had by the pressures explored by it. If you have been a victim or prey of the guided killer, do not feel humiliated since we all experience some kind of victimization at one time or another in our lives.

Most of us have a dark side. It becomes part of the human condition, however, agreed not to be well recognized. An undesirable reality, Dark Psychology borders us waiting patiently to strike. As this author has formerly stated, Dark Psychology encompasses all kinds of terrible and also violent habits. We need just look at the mindless cruelty to pets. Being a committed family pet fan, pet misuse to this writer is both ferocious and also psychopathic. As recent studies have suggested, animal misuse associates with a higher probability of devoting violence against humankind.

On the milder side of the Dark psychology is vandalism of other residential property or the increasing levels of violence in video games youngsters and teenagers advocate during the holiday. Destruction and a child's demand to play terrible computer games are mildly contrasted to overt violence, yet are explicit examples of this global human attribute this author's concept highlights. The vast majority of humankind denies and hides its existence, yet still, the components of Dark Psychology silently hide underneath the surface in all people.

It is universal and almost everywhere throughout society. Some religious beliefs specify it as a real entity they call Satan. Some cultures rely on the presence of evil forces as being the wrongdoers causing malicious activities.

This author tries to examine Dark Psychology's origin and nature to understand how the standard, well-socialized individual can wind up current, having dedicated a wrong no one can have forecasted. At any type of factor during the day and throughout the evening, wrongs caused by one human on one more are occurring because of the beginning of recorded history. Although horrible, it is incredible how decent people can perhaps participate in or enable such horrors to occur.

Thousands of these wrongs appear throughout the background. The holocaust throughout the Second World War and ethnic cleansing currently taking place in neighboring nations are a few instances. Experience, with the residues of what Dark Psychology has caused, is plentiful with cases. As explained above, Dark Psychology is alive and well and also requires a close examination. As you continue to discover the tenets and foundation of Dark Psychology, a cognitive structure of understanding will slowly establish.

Dark Continuum

The Dark Continuum is a crucial element to understand in your passage through the dark side of humankind. The Dark Continuum is a fictional conceptual line or concentric circles that all criminal, terrible, deviant, and vicious habits fall. The Dark Continuum includes thoughts, feelings, assumptions, and actions experienced or devoted by humans. The continuum varies from light to severe as well as from purposive to pointless.

Physical indications of Dark Psychology are up to the right of the Dark Continuum and extra severe. Emotional symptoms of Dark Psychology lie to the left of the continuum. However, they can be equally as harmful as physical acts. The Dark Continuum is not a range of intensity, ranging from poor to worse; however, it specifies typologies of victimization in the ideas and activities entailed. When this writer also broadens his thesis of the Dark Continuum, you will undoubtedly have a theoretical illustrated line depicting all forms of Dark Psychology ranging from moderate and purposive to extreme and purposeless.

Dark Variable

The Dark Element is specified as the realm, location, and potential in all of us and belongs to the human condition. This is one of the more abstract regards to Dark Psychology because it is so tough to highlight employing the created expression. According to an online dictionary, a variable is anything that contributes causally to an outcome, i.e., a variety of elements figured out the issue. This writer will undoubtedly attempt to theorize for you in a big way how Dark Aspect appears like an equation.

The Dark Aspect is not a mathematical formula, but a theoretical one. The Dark Element is a collection of occasions that a person experiences, enhancing their probability of participating in predacious habits. Although research study has suggested that youngsters who mature in violent homes become abusers themselves, this does not imply all mistreated children expand to end up being violent transgressors. This is merely one element of a wide range of experiences and scenarios contributing to the Dark Variable.

The number of components that are involved in the Dark Factor equation is enormous. It is not the number of aspects creating Dark Element to come to be extreme. Yet, the impact those experiences carry on an individual's subjective processing makes the Dark Aspect hazardous. Some of these aspects consist of genes, family member's characteristics, emotional knowledge, peer acceptance, personal handling, developmental turning points, and experiences.

Dark Singularity

The Dark Singularity is an academic principle comparable to the interpretation of singularity in the middle of a black hole. When this writer illustrates the concept of the Dark Selfhood, he makes use of astronomy as well as cosmology as an allegory to define this principle. In astrophysics, the singularity is the outright center of a black hole that is unbelievably tiny yet thick in mass beyond mathematical comprehension. The theory recommends that the uniqueness is so dense and powerful, contemporary laws of physics and their mathematical equations come to be knotted.

A black hole is the massive expanse of room bordering the singularity; therefore, abundant light cannot leave its grip. At the center of all galaxies, the Milky Way is an all-powerful great void with a considerably small singularity at its facility chock packed with remarkable energy. The Dark Singularity, as it puts on Dark Psychology, is the absolute center of the Dark Psychology world. Simply put, the Dark Selfhood is constructed from immaculate evil & unadulterated pure malevolence. Likewise, part of the human condition is the Dark Singularity that no person ever reaches. The person who comes closest to this is the innovative & extreme psychotic who preys on others with minimal inspiration or objective for his activities.

Since all behavior is purposive, the Dark Selfhood is an ideal destination never got to. The Dark Selfhood is come close to, yet without arrival. The center of Dark Selfhood is finest explained as "Predators That Victim without Purpose." The closer a person approaches the Dark Selfhood, the lot more horrendous and sinister their actions come to be. At the same time, their modus becomes much less deliberate. As mentioned, this is an abstract principle that this author will layout in his later works.

A psychological and also thoughtful tenet to understand when venturing to picture cognitively, the Dark Singularity, is that all behavior is purposive. This writer was honored to have finished his postgraduate degree in the mid-1990s at the Adler College in Chicago, Illinois. Alfred Adler was a Millennium medical doctor and a psychotherapist who was a modern of Sigmund Freud, Carl Jung, and an incredible philosopher.

Via this author's studies, he understood hold of most of Adler's theories. To now, this writer translates his world as defined by Alfred Adler, this fantastic clinical physician and psychotherapist. Adler had several concepts of human habits. This author also incorporated many of them throughout his building of Dark Psychology. The three most valuable ideas from Adler for developing the concept are as follows.

CHAPTER 26:

How to Use Dark Psychology to Succeed at Work

The main reason many people want to learn about dark psychology is that they want to do better in their careers. They aren't content working the job they already have—they want to prove themselves capable of more.

But somewhere along the way, we figure out the truth: that getting ahead in our careers isn't necessarily a matter of skill, but manipulation and persuasion. As you know, dark psychology is the best and most legitimate way to learn these skills, and now it's time to learn how to use them specifically in a work setting.

We have to think harder about how we interact with our co-workers. For instance, let's say we have a female early 20—something analyst in a post-graduation down cycle who has encountered many challenges both professionally and personally since starting work a few years ago.

She frequently finds herself wanting to connect with people who are perceived to be more advanced in their careers or whose interests are different from her own. Identifying why you are attracted to certain people is a valuable skill for early-career practitioners. It likely contributes to her success as an analyst.

Personality is an especially crucial subject for the workplace context because it is an environment where you have to interact with many different kinds of people, many of whom—you will soon find out—you don't know that well as people.

Dark psychology is broader than neurolinguistics programming, but NLP is where all of our tools and techniques of deep communication and manipulation come from. NLP is where the three big steps of manipulation and mind control originate from: Establish your state control and perceptual sharpness, imitate the unconscious cues of communication of your subject so that they incorporate you into their mind, and use one of the techniques to get them to change their ideas or behavior.

People constantly think without even realizing it because most thought is unconscious. NLP is how we take advantage of the unconscious nature of most thought to tell people's minds to change in the structure before they even know it.

NLP's topic is important for discussing personalities in the workplace because NLP has five main categories for the kinds of personalities people have. In the jargon of NLP, these "personalities" are called Meta programs. You would do well to identify the important people at your workplace within these Meta programs. Take advantage of your perceptual sharpness to ascertain this information.

As we have told you before, getting information about the subject is everything. But it is also true that our brains need to sort all the information we get into categories to better understand the world. These Meta programs do that job for you.

Meta programs are more useful than personalities because they are more objective. They also focus on the motivations people have and how they use logic, rather than on their mannerisms or less important patterns of behavior. Meta programs do not simply describe how much you like attention or how nervous or relaxed you are—you may notice some aspects of each Meta program that overlap with these traits, but Meta programs are much more specific than these less useful terms.

These NLP-styled personalities are not only a way for you to get more information about your co-workers. Remember the second step of NLP's mind-reading and manipulation: you have to imitate the communications cues the subject shows you. When you do this, you make them unconsciously see you as being like themselves. That means if you take on the traits of your co-worker's Meta program, you make it easier for you to succeed in this step.

The last thing for you to know about Meta programs, in general, is that they are sorted in dichotomies. A dichotomy is a contrast between two items that are different. But while you should choose just one from each dichotomy in each Meta program, you must remember that people are not as simple as being A or B. Any time we have a dichotomy—in any situation—picking one of the two is just a category you can use to simplify things and think of them differently. But you should not think of them as being always or exclusively one of the two. People are much more complex than this.

Our first Meta program is between the dichotomy of options and procedures. People who are on the options Meta program don't like being limited or being told what to do. They want as much freedom as possible, and they like to think about things from a general perspective rather than getting in the weeds. On the other hand, people on procedures need to understand every small detail whenever they get into something new. Procedures people hate the feeling that there is something they are missing. When detail is skipped, they fear they are missing something important.

The second Meta program is external and internal. This Meta program is concerned with people's incentives. External people want to be told by others when they do good work, and they want to be told when they do bad work, too. Internal people don't want to get outside opinions about their work, though. They feel they know when their work is good or not, and hearing what other people think is just a bother.

The third dichotomy in Meta programs is proactive and reactive. These Meta programs describe how someone deals with the future. Reactive people look at a calendar and are always thinking about how the work they are doing now fits into the picture of all of their work. This can be a hindrance because they think so much about planning that they lose sight of what they are trying to do right now. Proactive people, on the other hand, hate thinking about the future or planning ahead. They only care about the here and now.

Our second-to-last is toward and away. This Meta program is about goals and deterrents. All of us have things we look forward to in the future, but people are chiefly concerned about their goals, and they don't look behind them at all. Away people are the exact opposite of this. They can have issues looking ahead because they spend so much time thinking about what is behind them.

Finally, we have sameness and difference. Sameness people have a love for familiarity: they spend their time around things they already know. Things they don't know them fearful, so these people avoid them at all costs. On the other hand, different people are always craving new experiences, meeting new people, eating new foods, and so on. If there is something they haven't experience yet, different people want to experience it.

These are the five big dichotomies in Meta programs. Whoever the co-worker is who you want to use our dark psychology tricks on will want to sort them into these Meta programs. Now, when you use the Aristotelian technique of envisioning the future, you have a more objective stand-in for the person you will interact with.

When we imagine someone in our heads, it isn't always accurate to how they are. NLP's Meta programs are so useful because they make us think carefully about our subject's kind of person.

Meta programs are particularly good for the work environment because they force us to think about the people we work with more objectively. When you do Step 1 and prepare to get into the co-worker's mind with Step 2, you can use these Meta programs to paint a fuller picture of who you will use dark psychology on.

Since these are often just people: we interact with exclusively in work environments, we can be surprised by how little we might know about them from a Meta program standpoint. If you are honest with yourself as you sort them into these dichotomies, you might realize you don't know very much about them at all. When this turns out to be the case, don't just go along with the dark psychology technique anyway. There is no point in doing this when it won't work anyway—you can't adapt to the social cues of a person you don't even know yet.

That's why from here, you will have to do more intel-gathering on them first before you can even move on to Step 1. Step 1 can't successfully happen until you know the person and how they fit into all the Meta programs. Until you do that, you won't be able to properly imagine your interactions with them for Steps 2 and 3.

With that said, after you get to know the co-workers' Meta programs, let your senses do all the work in perceptual sharpness, use our exercises to prepare your state control, and imagine the interaction in your imagination, you are ready for Step 2.

However, some techniques seem tailor-made for use in the work setting. We will go over these before moving onto our big lesson on neurolinguistics programming in psychology.

We will cover three big dark psychology techniques for the workplace before diving into the world of NLP. Social framing is a technique in which we paint a picture for the subject where adopting a certain behavior or idea will help them with social climbing.

That's why framing the truth about the subject's social environment is such a powerful tool for manipulating and mind-controlling people. As long as we make them believe they get a social reward for doing what we say, they will jump at the opportunity.

[177]

CHAPTER 27:

Dangers of Dark Psychology

Dark Psychology might be a new field of study, but the concept has been around far longer than psychological researchers can pinpoint. They have discovered that everyone sits on the Dark Spectrum, some barely ever touching the dark sides of their brains, while others are completely immersed in it. On the one hand, it's just like everything else in life, if you know that the possibility for these tendencies is there, you will be better equipped to handle them if your mind begins to wander in that direction. Simultaneously, the idea that our brains can go that dark and deep into manipulative and dangerous behavior is frightening.

In everyday life, most people go through the motions, have goals, set up pathways to their goals, and work to get there. There is no real thought of deception and manipulation. However, the fact that it sits so close to the surface will make you think twice about your decisions and others who make decisions that can negatively impact you. While you may not be worried about your conscious behavior, you can't control the others around you.

The Dark Spectrum may be described as a line to some psychologists or like the petals on a flower to others, but either way, we all fall somewhere in that spectrum. It is vital to not only take a good look at yourself but at the people in your life as well. Where do they fall on this spectrum? What is their D-Factor? It may be something you've never thought about before but now brings some serious issues to mind.

Regardless of what the spectrum says, you are in control of your behavior and decisions. You hold the key to just how dark you want to be. Maybe you enjoy the dark side of the force, but maybe it scares you, as it should. Manipulation and extreme deception are harmful, not just to you and to the aggressor but also to society. We evolve with the times, and society dictates many of our actions.

Think about the last time you were under extreme stress. Think about the way you felt, some of the thoughts that circulated through your mind. Were you in total control of yourself? Did you find yourself slipping further down the spectrum? It's only natural to react to stress, anger, and negative emotion with an air of caution. But it's unfortunately also natural to want revenge. To want to take an easy route to the things we want in our lives. When we see an opportunity to have what we want, it's hard to turn away from that, even if it means putting someone else down in the process. It's also important in times like those to think about what you are capable of. And if you believe you are capable of things nefarious and dark, ask yourself if you want to be that person. Those are the perfect time to reach out to people that care about you. Or reach out to a professional who can help you through these thoughts. There is no reason to give in to your dark psyche just because it's there. You want to be in control of your life, which means you don't want to control others or be controlled by someone else. Once you have a really good grasp on your level of capabilities, it is important to remember that not everyone is like you. From Ted Bundy to the guy who attempts to control you in a relationship, the spectrum is huge but real. If there was one Ted Bundy, there are more, hiding in someone's deep dark psyche. They may never bring him to light, but remember the possibilities are there.

None of this is said to frighten you or create a negative outlook on the world or other people. It is there to remind you that we are all capable of both light and dark. It is there to show you that Dark Psychology can be dangerous if used in the wrong way. So, keep your eyes open, be careful with the people you let in your life, and most importantly, take care of your mental health. It is truly what can make or break your future. There are very few times we witness the bad guy truly win in the end.

Everyday Professions That Use Dark Psychology

We touched on the infinite depth that the dark psyche can go. Still, we've only lightly touched on the dark psychology used on an everyday basis all around us. There are numerous professions where people use these exact tactics to get what they want. Hopefully, if you are in one of these professions, you take heed and carefully tread as the dark psyche can often come back and bite you when you're least expecting it.

Lawyers

Lawyers use tactics of manipulation, deceit, lies, deception, and many others in their daily line of work. The entire point of their job is to convince others of someone's guilt or innocence. Often it's a stretch to do that, and they have to resort to these tactics to convince the judge or jury so they can get their way. There are a lot of examples of bribery within the judicial system as well.

Doctors

You may be thinking that doctors are there to help people, not hurt them. And in most instances, this is true. But outside of actual diagnosis, there is a ring of pharmaceutical companies just itching for new clients. There is a reason that some doctors claim there is nothing good about natural medicine. It doesn't fill their pockets. Pharmaceutical companies bribe doctors all the time, pushing them to prescribe their medication to clients. This can easily lead to overmedicated people, people with the wrong medications, and a lack of quality healthcare for those that need it. It's the last thing we need to worry about when we get sick.

Athletes

How many times have we heard stories of athletes being disqualified for things such as steroid and drug abuse? But inside the game, there can be some serious issues as well. Taking down other players to the point of injury just to win a game. Doing dishonest things like deflating balls is another. Within the realm of athletes, we've seen murders, abusers, and rapists arrested every year. It makes you wonder whether the influx of dark psyche within the game affects the dark psyches when they hang up their uniforms for the night and go home.

Police Officers

Police officers face serious backlash from the community in recent years between the beatings and the senseless killings. Within the cycle of this type of job comes an extreme amount of power over people, their inability to hold that power at a reasonable level can be their dark psyches at work. There have been stories of murders, beatings, rapes, bribery, and deception within the police departments, but nothing ever seems to change.

Politicians

Did I even need to list politicians? The list of Machiavellian style deceit, trickery, bribery, lies, deception, manipulation, and worse, is outrageous inside our political system.

There are very few politicians in history that are clear from this type of judgment. They have twisted, jerked around, and manipulated the public for so long that most of us just try to pick the least evil out of them to support.

Where money lies, so will a plethora of dark psyches. Politics seem to be a magnet for these types of people. There is power, and there is money. What more could a dark psyche ask for?

Disturbing Dark Psychology Studies

In the 1960s, a psychologist by the name of Stanley Milgram began studying the psychology of obedience. It was not, and continues not to be, a highly researched area of psychology. To study the human behavior behind the theory of obedience, he put together a study that looked more like an experiment of will. This study went on to be one of the most controversial pieces of research in psychological history.

Milgram took his volunteers to a lab where he explained that they would participate in a study about learning. Each one was brought into the room one at a time and seat at a table with a microphone and a dial. The volunteers were then explained that there was, what he called, a 'learner' in the other room. They would be able to hear everything the learner did during this session. They were to clearly and concisely ask the learner the pre-scripted questions they were given using their microphones. At the time, the volunteers did not know the learner was a paid actor. They were then told that if the learner gave them the wrong answer, listening to him through the speaker would administer an electric shock. They would set the dial to the prescribed voltage and press the button. The dial was labeled from mild to fatal. During the process, an administrator stayed in the room with, dressed in a white lab coat, looking like part of the team. During the experiment, the learner began to give wrong answers to the questions that were being answered. Even when the volunteer hesitated, the administrator demanded that they continue giving the shocks to the learner, increasing the severity with each one. They could hear the learner's screams of pain through the speakers. If the volunteer refused, they were then instructed to continue with the following change of script:

- Please continue.

- The experiment requires that you continue.

- You must continue.

At that point, what would you do as a volunteer? During that experiment, a shocking sixty-five percent of the volunteers gave the learner the fatal shock. Even those that refused to do it, and demanded the experiment end immediately, never checked on whether the learner was okay or not. When they reviewed the volunteers' comments after they had been explained the experiment, most felt remorse. It even claimed they were not that kind of person. The problem was, they were fearful of the administrator. It was a cruel study but important to demonstrate the dark psyche's appearance in times of extreme duress. Milgram used his studies to explain why the Nazi soldiers in World War 2 were so loyal to the cause.

The second study is equally as scary. Philip Zimbardo, in the 1970s, ran an experiment called the Stanford Prison Experiment. The experiment's entire premise was to prove that people were manipulated into behaving in evil or scary ways very easily. A group of University students volunteered for the experiment, and the basement of the University was made to look and feel like a real prison. Randomly, people were chosen to either be guards or inmates. While the study never fully revealed what happened in the basement, the study was cut from a two-week-long study to only six days. It was later said that the guards began acting in sadistic manners, only to find they completely appalled when the project was pulled.

Conclusion

People are never as simple as their surfaces. There is always more going on underneath. Should you be troubled by this? If you've lived your life buying the smiling faces and seemingly straightforward motives of your friends and associates, should this hidden reservoir of dark psychology cause you consternation? I don't think so. By letting people be complicated, we're validating them as people. We're letting them exist in our estimations at a higher level than the cardboard cutouts we imagined. There's something a little condescending about imagining a human being as being one-dimensional, a background character in our own lives. Not – everyone is the hero of their own story, and everyone is complicated. We do them a great service by recognizing this. In acknowledging it, we take the first step towards living in a more complex, more adult, and ultimately more fulfilling world.

We have talked about the difference between persuasion and manipulation. Both are methods of convincing, of making an argument. However, the difference is that while the persuader plays fair, winning, and argues with logic and appeals, the manipulator acts dishonestly and without the best interests of their audience in mind. Manipulation is something anyone can but can be easier, and pathological for those with certain deviant personality types. These include narcissists, whose self-centered worldview overpowers everything else, sociopaths, who cannot feel empathy, and psychotics, who live in worlds of delusion. Manipulators can be dangerous to others' well-being, and relationships with them can be toxic and difficult to escape. We've also talked about the specific techniques employed by manipulators, with an extended case study into the methods used by cold readers and other false psychic phenomena purveyors.

The biggest mistake people make is to assume that other people are simple. That they are one-note. As we've seen, people put on masks. It's natural. You do it, and I do as well. You want to decide what you reveal to the world and what you withhold. But remember, if you're doing it, so is everyone else. Look around you. Some people are smiling, some might have neutral expressions. Maybe you see someone who seems noticeably mad. Each of these people has pain. Deep pain. Maybe it is carried over from childhood. Maybe it finds its source in the disappointments of adulthood, in the fact that reality never lives up to the expectations we start with. Maybe they bury it. Maybe they share it with a therapist. Maybe they've dealt with it and moved on. Or maybe it has taken them over, driven them to drugs or alcohol, or given those issues with mental illness, or made it difficult to form strong relationships. Maybe they cry themselves to sleep every night. But everyone has a dark side.

How can you exist in this world of masks, where you never can know for sure what lurks behind them? A friendly coworker could be a secret manipulator? A potential romantic interest could be an incompatible mess of complex unprocessed trauma. You never know.

The most important first step, which we talked about at some length, is protecting yourself. One way to do this is to deal with your dark impulses. Don't bottle it up. Don't blame yourself. Don't deny it. Deal with it. Admitting that you are complex, and accepting that this is simply part of being human, will allow you to exist as a more fully integrated and holistically functioning human being. The happiest people are not those who have dealt with the least hardship. They are those who have a deal with hardship the best. The other important way to protect you is to be aware of the masks of others. No, you don't have to live in fear of the monster hiding behind the smiling face, but it is important to do your due diligence. Don't assume that the surface is the whole story. It never is. Never, especially when dealing with new people, be smart and remain observant. And once you feel that you have gathered enough information to understand that this person can be trusted, and you begin to let your guard down, don't throw it all away be hiding behind masks of your own. True trust, true love, truly functional relationships are those in which we can be honest with each other. When we can let each other see behind our masks to realize people that live behind them fully.

Life is a struggle. Don't expect to get it all right. Don't expect ever to perfect your life, relationships, or personality. The best we can do is to keep diligently trying, cautiously, confidently, optimistically, with open eyes and open hearts.

www.ingramcontent.com/pod-product-compliance
Lightning Source LLC
Chambersburg PA
CBHW061759250726
48657CB00001B/193